The Rook's Guide to C++

26 November 2013

Printed in the United States of America

First edition: November 2013

ISBN 978-1-304-66105-0

Rook's Guide Press
19 Black Road
Berlin, VT 05602
http://rooksguide.org

Preface

What you are reading is the first of what I hope to be many ever-improving iterations of a useful C++ textbook. We've gone fairly quickly from whim to print on an all-volunteer basis, and as a result, there are many things that I'd add and change if I had an infinite amount of time in my schedule. The vast majority of the contents were written in less than 36 hours by 25 students (mostly freshmen!) at Norwich University over a long weekend. Some of it is mine, and some was added by our crack team of technical editors as we translated sleep-deprived poor grammar into sleep-deprived better grammar.

Where it goes from here is mostly up to you! If there's a section that's missing or in need of clarification, please take a bit of time and make those changes. If you don't want to bother yourself with the GitHub repository, send me your additions and modifications directly.

I want to first thank my family for the time I didn't spend with them on the writing weekend and throughout the summer when I was editing and typesetting. I promise I won't do this next summer!

My next thanks go out to the technical editors and typesetters, without whom you would have a much uglier book. Thanks to Ted Rolle for building the initial LaTeX framework and to Matt Jadud for the incredibly helpful pointers on how to manage the pile of typesetting files in a collaborative environment. I also thank Craig Robbins and Levi Schuck, who, on different sides of the planet, managed to contribute extensively to the heavy lifting of getting the book into the shape it's in now. If we ever meet, I owe you a beer or whatever you're having!

I also would like to thank all of the Kickstarter backers not only for the money which made this possible, but for reinforcing the idea that this is a worthwhile contribution to the community. Peter Stephenson and Andrew Pedley also contributed food directly over the textbook writing hackathon weekend, and without them we'd never have gotten our saturated fat quota! (Note to future project leaders: there's nothing that gets a bunch of college students who are generally lukewarm about programming to write a textbook like free food. It didn't even matter what the food was. Really.)

Thanks to Matt Russo for shooting the video and organizing the media and social networking efforts with the Kickstarter project through the writing weekend.

Special thanks to Allyson LeFebvre[1] for the textbook photography, several diagrams, and the extensive search through the semifinal textbook that turned up a bunch of mistakes that I missed.

And my last (and not at all least) thanks go out to all the students who showed up in person or digitally. And without getting too grandiose, you remind us all that we can make the world better by showing up. Keep showing up!

Jeremy
jeremyhansen@acm.org
26 November 2013

---

[1]That's "la-fave", everyone

Contents

License

Dramatis Personæ

Managing Editor:
> Jeremy A. Hansen, PhD, CISSP

Technical Editing & Typesetting:
> Jeremy A. Hansen
>
> Matt Jadud, PhD
>
> Craig D. Robbins
>
> Theodore M. Rolle, Jr.
>
> Levi Schuck

Media & Outreach:
> Matthew E. Russo

Cover Art & Graphic Design:
> Allyson E. LeFebvre

Content Authors:
> Tyler Atkinson, Troy M. Dundas, Connor J. Fortune, Jeremy A. Hansen, Scott T. Heimann, Benjamin J. Jones, Michelle Kellerman, Michael E. Kirl, Zachary LeBlanc, Allyson E. LeFebvre, Gerard O. McEleney, Phung P. Pham, Megan Rioux, Alex Robinson, Kyle R. Robinson-O'Brien, Jesse A. Rodimon, Matthew E. Russo, Yosary Silvestre, Dale R. Stevens, Ryan S. Sutherland, James M. Verderico, Christian J. Vergnes, Rebecca Weaver, Richard Z. Wells, and Branden M. Wilson.

Funding & Support:
> Peter Stephenson, PhD, VSM, CISSP, CISM, FICAF, LPI at the Norwich University Center for Advanced Computing & Digital Forensics
>
> Andrew Pedley at Depot Square Pizza

Kickstarter contributors:

Nathan Adams, Chris Aldrich, Jay Anderson, Kent Archie, Erik Arvedson, Astrolox, Phoebe Ayers, Papa Joe Barr, Julia Benson-Slaughter, Georgia Perimeter College, Patrick Berthon, Francis Bolduc, Greg Borenstein, Patrick Breen, Igor Bronshteyn, Valdemar Bučilko, Ross Buckley, Nikita Burtsev, Jakob Bysewski, David Camara, Dave M. Campbell, Brian V. Campbell III, S. Canero, Serge Canizares, Andrew Carlberg, Casey B. Cessnun, Winston Chow, W. Jesse Clements, Greg Crawford, Sean Cristofori, Jordan G Cundiff, Michael David, Joseph Davies, Ashley Davis, David C. Dean, DJS, Carlton Doc Dodd, Phil Dodds, Dominic, Sankar Dorai, dryack, Matt DuHarte, Brandon Duong, Van Van Duong, Daniel Egger, Chris Fabian, Jorge F. Falcon, Tek Francis, Fuchsi, Steve Gannon, Michael Gaskins, Gavlig, Adam Gibson, Russell E. Gibson, Goldenwyrm, James Green, Brian J. Green, Casey Grooms, Vitalik Gruntkovskiy, Vegar Guldal, Felix Gutbrodt, Jeremy Gwinnup, Beau T. Hahn, Paul R. Harms - Norwich 1975, Corey H. Hart, MBA, Aaron A. Haviland, Josh Heffner, Greg Holland, Henry Howard, Mark V Howe, Ivaliy Ivanov, Matt Jadud, Joseph Jaoudi, Tim R. Johnson, Ibi-Wan Kentobi, Mark King, Mitchell Kogut III, Sigmund Kopperud, Michael Korolev, Jamie Kosoy, Aria Kraft, Alexander Týr Kristjánsson, Richard Kutscher, Eric Laberge, John Lagerquist, Philip Lawrence, Mark Brent Lee, John and Nancy LeFebvre, Nevin :-) Liber, Jonathan Lindquist, Thomas Lockney, Stuart A. MacGillivray, Dr. Pedro Maciel, Troels Holstein Madsen, William Marone, Fred Mastropasqua, Miles Mawyer, michael mazzello, Ryan McDonough, Matthew McFadden, John McIntosh II, Sean McNamara, mdsaravanan, Brandon Meskimen, Andrew Mike, G.F. Miller IV, Marcus Millin, Salvador Torres Morales, Danny Morgan, Ken Moulton, Aaron Murray, mvi, Jon Nebenfuhr, Philip K. Nicholson, chris nielsen, Pontus Nilsson, Mike Noble, Aleksander R. Nordgarden-Rødner, Greg O'Hanlon, Doug Otto, Randy Padawer, Ph.D., J Palmer, Tasos Papastylianou, Paul, James Pearson-Kirk, Matthew Peterson, Grigory Petrov, pezmanlou, Joachim Pileborg, Kyle Pinches, pkh, Mary Purdey, Marshall Reeves, Matthew Ringman, Craig D. Robbins, Antonio Rodriguez, Armando Emanuel Roggio, Victor Suarez Rovere, Christian Sandberg, Jaymes Sattler, Paolo Scalia, Patrice Scheidt, Daniel Schmitt, Levi Schuck, Raman Sharma_Himachali, Michael Shashoua, Daniel Shiffman, Clay Shirky, sillygoatgirl, Kevin J. Slonka, Brian Smith, Hazel Smith & Rebecca Twigg, Andrey Soplevenko, Kasper Souren, Derek A. Spangler, Speckman, Kellan St.Louis, Nick Stefanou, Steve, Andrew Stewart, Jeremy Sturdivant, Cyrille Tabary, Adam 8T Tannir, M Taylor, Telecat Productions, Aron Temkin, Mitchell Tilbrook, Nathan Tolbert, Devin M. Tomlinson - Vermont Born, Todd Trimble, Michiel van Slobbe, James A. Velez, Marco Verdecchia, David Walter, Lothar Werzinger, Wayne West, Sean Whaley '05 & M'08, Mark Wheeler, Tommy Widenflycht, Dylan Widis, Tony Williamitis, Adam M. Williams, Stephen D. Williams, Dylan Wilson, Wesley Wiser, wizzy, Sam Wright, Janet Hong Yam, and Jy Yaworski.

Chapter 1

History

Developed by Bjarne Stroustrup, C++ has become one of the most popular programming languages in the world. Originally, it was designed as an improvement upon the C language, which was developed by Bell Labs. Developed in the early 1970s, C's name is derived from the B programming language, which in turn was derived from the BCPL language. C gained a large following, in part due to its use in the development of the UNIX operating system. Due to both its popularity and the number of versions on the market, an American National Standards Institute (ANSI) committee was formed in 1982 to create a standard for the C language, which was adopted in 1989.

Stroustrup began with the idea that object oriented programming would be an important addition to C, and created C with Classes. In 1983, Stroustrup's contributions officially became known as C++, its name stemming from C and adding the ++ (increment) operator. It wasn't until 1998 that the international standard for C++ was established.

Since then, most changes have been minor. In 2005, a report was released by the ISO on features that were intended to be included in the next version of C++. The early versions of this became known as C++0x, until 2011, when the C++11 standard was released by the ISO.

In this book, we'll favor older techniques, pre-C++11. When C++11 features are discussed, they will be pointed out as such. While not all of the new features are discussed, we will be trying our best to explain them as we go.

Chapter 2

Variables

Variables are extremely important to every programmer - they will be a critical part of your programming toolkit regardless of the language you use. Very simply put, a variable is a space in memory that can store some range of values. Some of the basic data types are shown in Table 2.1. For a deeper discussion of data types, refer to Chapter 9.

`int`	Short for integer; stores whole numbers
`char`	Short for character; stores a single letter, digit, or symbol
`bool`	Short for Boolean; stores `true` or `false`
`float`	Short for floating point number; stores numbers with fractional parts
`double`	Short for double precision floating point number; stores bigger numbers with bigger fractional parts than `float`

Table 2.1: A few basic data types

2.1   How do I decide which data type I need?

What you can do with a variable depends on the type of data they contain. For instance, you can't store the number 100000 in a char because a char stores only character data. To store 100000 the programmer should use an int. If you think you are dealing with numbers that have fractional parts, you need at least a float. You generally want to use the smallest variable type that will get your job done. Simply put, if it is a round number, int works fine; if it's a true or false, use bool; for a letter, use char; for fractional numbers, use float; for a really big number or a number with many digits after the decimal point, use double.

2.2   Identifiers

Now we have an idea of what types of variables we will use in the program. How do we have the program differentiate between multiple ints, chars, or doubles? We have to name them! The name we use will give the variable an identity, so it's known as an **identifier**. An identifier can be almost anything you'd like, provided the identifier does not begin with a number or symbol.[1] Remember that the variable name can only be one word long. You may use a an underscore to replace a space if you so desire, and note that C++ is case sensitive. That is, testresults, TestResults, and Test_Results are all different identifiers.

2.3   Declaring a Variable

The line of code that creates a variable is called a **declaration**. A declaration is the program telling the computer "save a place in memory for me with this name."

A declaration for an integer variable named myVariable looks like this:

```
int  myVariable ;
```

The specific **syntax**—the set of grammatical rules for the language—is important to follow when declaring variables. Notice that the first part (int) is the data type of the variable. The second part is the identifier (myVariable), or variable name. The last part is the semicolon (;) which signifies the end of a statement. You can think of the semicolon in C++ as equivalent to a period at the end of a sentence;

---

[1]There are a few exceptions, including those words that describe data types (as in the table above) and other keywords such as if and while, which you'll learn about in later chapters.

it is the end of a complete thought. Note that you may declare several variables of the same data type together. Consider this example:

```
int x, y, z;
double a;
```

The above example creates three variables of type `int` named x, y, and z and one variable of type `double` named a.

2.4 Initializing Variables

Values can be immediately assigned to a variable at the time of its declaration. This is known as **initializing** a variable. To do this, the variable's name is followed by an equals sign (=, the **assignment operator**), the value, and a semicolon. Consider this example:

```
int x = 20;
double a = 2.2;
```

Note that uninitialized variables can cause problems if they are used anywhere before they are assigned a value. When a variable is declared, it contains whatever was already in that space of memory, which can give them unpredictable values. This means that is is often a good idea to initialize variables to some sensible initial value when they are declared.

2.5 Assignment Statements

An assignment statement is a method of assigning a value to a variable after it has been declared. All assignment statements have the variable being assigned the value on the left side of an equals sign and the value to assign on the right side. Note that the expression on the right side of the assignment may contain arithmetic operations such as multiplication, division, addition, and subtraction, or even other variables. Consider the following example:

```
int a = 1, b = 2, x = 0, y = 0;
x = a + b;
y = x;
```

2.6 Review Questions

1. Declare two variables of type int and initialize them to an appropriate value.

2. Declare three integer variables: sum, a, b. Initialize the variables a and b to an appropriate integer and use an assignment statement to assign sum the result of a plus b.

3. Declare a double variable called number and initialize it to 13.6.

4. Create a program in which 3 variables are declared. Create one float named myFloat, one int named myInt, and one double named my-Double. Initialize them to 3.14, 3, and 3.14159, respectively.

2.7 Review Answers

1. int a = 6;
   int b = 0;

2. int sum, a = 6, b = 0;
   sum = a + b;

3. double number = 13.6;

4.
```
int main ()
{
   float myFloat = 3.14;
   int myInt = 3;
   double myDouble = 3.14159;

   return 0;
}
```

2.8 Further Reading

- http://www.cplusplus.com/doc/tutorial/variables/
- http://www.tutorialspoint.com/cplusplus/cpp_variable_types.htm

Chapter 3

Literals and Constants

3.1 Literals

A literal is a value outside of a variable such as 5, 9, 103, and -21. Each of those is an int, but a literal can be of any data type. The point is, these are values that the C++ compiler already recognizes, and can't be changed. In other words, you can't convince the compiler to give the literal 3 the value of 4, because 3 is constant. Table 3.1 contains a few examples.

3.2 Declared Constants

We call a variable whose value we cannot change a constant. After you declare a constant, you are unable to change it, no matter what. The difference between declaring a normal variable and a constant is that we simply place the keyword const before the data type in the declaration. This indicates whatever variable and type that follows the const will be a constant and cannot be changed. Since it is a constant, we will also need to initialize the value at the time we declare the variable. Here is an example (we cover the cout object shortly in Chapter 5):

```
const float pi = 3.14;
float radius = 5, area;

area = radius * radius * pi;
cout << area; // outputs 78.5
```

Literal value	Data Type
123.45f	float
13.8903	double
-389283220.342423	double
49e-8	double
12	int
12u	unsigned int
'x'	char
"text"	string
true	bool
false	bool

Table 3.1: Examples of a few literals

3.3 Review Questions

1. Describe the difference between literals and declared constants. When would a declared constant be more useful than a literal constant?

2. What is the difference between a normal variable and a constant?

3. Build a program in C++ that does the following:

    (a) Declare a double variable named Feet. Initialize it to your height.

    (b) Declare a double constant named MetersPerFoot, with the value of 0.3048.

    (c) Declare a double variable named Meters. Set it to Feet multiplied by MetersPerFoot.

4. Create a program that displays the diameter and area of a circle for any given radius. Use a const float to represent π.

3.4 Review Answers

1. A literal is a value not stored in a variable; a constant is an unchanging value stored in a variable.

2. Normal variables can be changed or overwritten; constants cannot be changed or overwritten.

3.

```
double  Feet  5.5;
const  double  MetersPerFoot  =  .3048;
double  Meters  =  Feet  *  MetersPerFoot;
```

4.

```
float  radius  =  5;
const  float  pi  =  3.14159
double  diameter,  area;
diameter  =  radius  *  2;
area  =  pi  *  (radius  *  radius)
```

Chapter 4

Assignments

Assignments are a way for a user or a programmer to assign a value to a variable. The way we assign a value to a variable in C++ is different from how we might do it in math. In mathematics we are allowed to say that x = 3 or 3 = x, but in C++ the only acceptable way to assign the value of 3 to x is to type x = 3.

The = in the expression x = 3 is known as an **assignment operator**. This allows the program to set a variable's value depending on its type. Here are some examples of setting a value to different types of variables:

```
int x = 4;
char alpha = 'A';
string word = "Alpha";
float y = 3.14;
```

We are able to declare variables and assign a value to those variables immediately by using the assignment operator. When we assign literal values to variables of type char, the value must be surrounded by single quotes (for example, 'A'). When we assign values to variables of type string, the literal value must be surrounded by double quotes (for example, "Alpha"). We do not have to initialize the values of the variables, however. We can set them later in the code like this:

```
int myVal;
//some code
myVal = 0;
```

In all of the lines of code in this section where a variable is set using the assignment operator, the "thing that is being given a value" is known as an **lvalue**, and the expression on the right that is being stored in the variable is known as the

11

rvalue. Literals such as 'A' or 3 can never be an lvalue. Aside from literals, the rvalue can consist of other variables, like this:

```
myVal = myVal2;
```

Even though myVal2 is a variable, we are only using the *value stored in the variable*, not the variable itself. For example, if myVal2 had a value of 6, myVal would then be assigned to the value 6 with the above code.

We can also store the results of an arithmetic expression in a variable like this:

```
myVal = 5 + 6;   // assigns myVal a value of 11
```

But we can't write

```
5 + 6 = myVal;   // ERROR!
```

since 5 + 6 doesn't refer to a place where we can store a value. We can also combine arithmetic expressions with variables as an rvalue like this:

```
myVal2 = 6;
myVal = 4 + myVal2;
```

In this case, the variable myVal would be assigned a value of 10 because the variable myVal2 was initialized to a value of 6, and 4 + 6 is 10. The value of myVal2 remains unchanged. Make sure that the variable myVal, the variable myVal2, and the literal 4 are of the same type. For example, the following code will result in an error:

```
int myValue = 4;
int yourVal;
string myString = "word";

yourVal = myValue + myString;
// Adding string to an int is
// probably not what you meant!
```

When we try to combine different variable types, the compiler will get very mad at us. Some exceptions to this rule are if we try to combine floats, ints, and doubles. These types have the ability to be combined (to a certain extent) because they are all numeric values. Both doubles and floats can hold values with a decimal point such as -3.14, 0.003, or 5.167289 whereas an int can only hold round values such as 2, -18, or 100. Refer to Chapter 9 for more information on converting between data types.

4.1 Review Questions

1. Which of the following is an incorrect way to assign a value to a variable x of type `int`?

    (a) `7 = x;`

    (b) `int x = 7;`

    (c) `int x(7);`

    (d) `x = 7;`

2. Which of the following is an incorrect way to assign a value to a variable of type `string`?

    (a) `string myString = "word";`

    (b) `string myString = 'word';`

    (c) `myString = "word";`

3. Is the following code incorrect? If so, why? If it is correct, why?

```
int  x  =  6,  y;
char  myChar  =  'x';
y  =  myChar  +  x;
```

4. Write a program that declares two `int` variables and two `double` variables. Add and subtract five from each of your declared integer variables. Then add and subtract 7.32 your `double` variables by 7.32. Then output each of your results to the screen.

4.2 Review Answers

1. **a.** When we store a value in a variable, the variable goes on the left of the assignment operator, and the value being stored in that variable goes to the right of the assignment operator.

2. **b.** String literals must be surrounded by double quotes, not single quotes; single quotes are used for single characters like `'b'`.

3. The code is incorrect. This will probably not produce the expected result it tries to add an `int` and a `char` and store that value in a variable of type `int`.

Chapter 5

Output

Output in C++ is done with the object cout ("console **out**put"). The object cout prints useful information to the screen for the user. For example, if we wanted to prompt the user with

Type in your name:

we would use cout. cout is extremely important when you are starting to learn C++ as it gives you the ability to display the current state of any variable and provide user feedback at any point in your program. Let's make a program that outputs something to the screen:

```
#include <iostream>
using namespace std;
int main()
{
    cout << "Go Cadets!";
    return 0;
}
```

The symbol << is called the **insertion operator** and is needed between cout and what you want to display to the screen. In this case, we are displaying a string literal "Go Cadets!". As you know, every statement in C++ ends with a semi-colon, and this one is no exception.

What if we want to print more, though?

```
#include <iostream>
using namespace std;
int main()
{
  cout << "Go Cadets!";
  cout << "You can do it!";
  return 0;
}
```

Try to compile and run that. It works, but it's not really the desired output. You should get:

`Go Cadets!You can do it!`

How do we get those on a different line? One of the ways we can do it is to use the object endl. endl means "**end line**", and is used when you want to end one line and start over on the next—it's like hitting enter on your keyboard. You will also need another redirect operator between the string literal and the endl. Putting all of this together looks like this:

```
#include <iostream>
using namespace std;
int main()
{
  cout << "Go Cadets!" << endl;
  cout << "You can do it!";
  return 0;
}
```

This prints:

`Go Cadets!`
`You can do it!`

That works a bit more as intended. Alternatively, we can combine the two lines that use cout into a single one like this:

```
cout << "Go Cadets!" << endl << "You can do it!";
```

Another way we can accomplish this, without needing another redirect operator, is with the special character '\n'. '\n' is a newline character, it prints a new line just like the endl object.

```
#include <iostream>
using namespace std;
int main()
{
    cout << "Go Cadets!\nYou can do it!";
    return 0;
}
```

This prints:
Go Cadets!
You can do it!

Another thing we can use with the console output object is the special character '\t'. Printing this character is the same as pressing the tab key on your keyboard, and is used for indentation and formatting. Let's look at an example that uses the newline character, the tab character, and some text:

```
#include <iostream>
using namespace std;
int main()
{
    cout << "\tGo Cadets!\nYou can do it!";
    return 0;
}
```

This code prints:
    Go Cadets!
You can do it!

We don't always have to output words the screen using cout. We can also print variables of type int, double, and float and can control the number of digits that appear after the decimal point. For example, if we had a variable that contained the value 3.14159265 we might only care about the first two numbers after the decimal point and just want to output 3.14 to the screen. We do that with the precision() member function. This function call will result in subsequent float or double variables being printed with the specified number of decimal places. In the following code, the number of digits is set to 2:

```
#include <iostream>
using namespace std;
int main()
{
    double num = 3.14159265;
    cout.precision(2);
    cout << num << endl;
}
```

This code prints:
3.14

To display data in a similar way as a spreadsheet, we can create a field of characters and set the number of characters in each field using the `width()` and `fill()` member functions. Notice the use of the `left` flag in the following code, which positions the output on the left side of the field; the default is for the output to be on the right side:

```cpp
#include <iostream>
using namespace std;
int main()
{
   cout << "Norwich" << endl;
   cout.width(15);
   cout << "University" << endl;
   cout.fill('*');
   cout.width(20);
   cout << left << "Corps of Cadets" << endl;
}
```

The above code prints:
```
Norwich
        University
Corps of Cadets*****
```

5.1   Review Questions

1. Which of the following is a correct way to output `Hello World` to the screen?

    (a) `output: "Hello World";`

    (b) `cout >> "Hello World";`

    (c) `cout << "Hello World";`

    (d) `console.output << "Hello World";`

2. Which of the following is a correct way to output `Hello!` to the screen on one line and `Goodbye!` to the screen on the next line?

    (a) `cout >> "Hello!" >> "Goodbye!";`

    (b) `output: "Hello!\nGoodbye!";`

    (c) `cout << "Hello!" << \n << "Goodbye!";`

    (d) `cout << "Hello!" << '\n' << "Goodbye!";`

3. Aside from the answer in the previous question, write two alternative ways of printing Hello! and Goodbye! to the screen on two different lines.

4. Write several lines of code using the width() and fill() functions in a main() that prints Programming! to the screen with 4 'x' characters printed after it.

5. Write code to output the values 124, 12.376, z, 1000000, and strings! as distinct values, separated by spaces.

6. What is the output of the following program?

```
#include <iostream>
#include <string>
using namespace std;
int main()
{
    string shirt = "maroon", pants = "blue";

    cout << shirt << " " << pants << endl;
    return 0;
}
```

5.2 Review Answers

1. c.

2. d.

3. `cout << "Hello!" << endl << "Goodbye!";` or
   `cout << "Hello!\nGoodbye!";`
   (other similar answers are possible)

4.
```
cout.fill('x');
cout.width(16);
cout << left << "Programming!";
```

5. `cout << 124 << " " << 12.376 << " z " << 1000000 << " strings!";`

6. `maroon blue`

5.3 Further Reading

- http://java-samples.com/showtutorial.php?tutorialid=245

- http://www.cplusplus.com/doc/tutorial/basic_io
- http://www.cplusplus.com/reference/ostream/ostream/
- http://www.cplusplus.com/doc/tutorial/functions/

Chapter 6

Input

When a programmer wants a user to enter data, such as the price of an item, he or she will use the `cin` object, pronounced "see-in", in conjunction with >>, the **extraction operator** in the program. Let us look at the following code:

```
#include <iostream>
using namespace std;
int main()
{
    int x = 0;
    cout << "Please enter a value for x: " << endl;
    cin >> x;
    return 0;
}
```

When you compile and run this code, here's what the output will look like:
```
Please enter a value for x:
```
As a user you may want to check the value that was entered. To do this, simply

add an additional cout statement like this:

```
#include <iostream>
using namespace std;
int main()
{
    int x = 0;
    cout << "Please enter a value for x: " << endl;
    cin >> x;
    cout << "The value of x is: " << x;
    return 0;
}
```

The output of this code is:

Please enter a value for x:

Suppose the user enters a value of 1 for x. The output that follows is:

The value of x is: 1

As you can see, the value displayed is the one entered. This can be a very useful technique in troubleshooting the values of variables throughout a program. Do not be afraid to insert additional cout statements throughout a program to check the values of variables when debugging. This can help in the debugging process and speed up catching errors.

If you want to have a user input more than one value, just repeat the code for each individual variable:

```
#include <iostream>
using namespace std;
int main()
{
    int x = 0;
    int y = 0;

    cout << "Please enter a value for x: " << endl;
    cin >> x;
    cout << "Please enter a value for y: " << endl;
    cin >> y;
    cout << "The value of x is: " << x << endl;
    cout << "The value of y is: " << y << endl;
    return 0;
}
```

We can't always trust that the user will input the correct data into a variable. For example, if a user was prompted to input an age into a variable of type int but typed the character z, the program would not behave properly because the user entered the wrong data type. We can check for improper input like this by using the `cin.fail()` function in a conditional statement. Look at the following code:

```
#include <iostream>
using namespace std;
int main()
{
    int x = 0;
    int y = 0;

    cout << "Please enter a value for x: " << endl;
    cin >> x;
    if (cin.fail())
    {
        cout << "That is not a valid data type!";
    }
}
```

This introduction to `cin` statements is only the beginning. They will get slightly more complicated after we introduce `strings`, arrays, and overloaded operators.

6.1 Review Questions

1. Which of the following numbered lines of code are proper `cin` statements?

```
#include <iostream>
using namespace std;
int main()
{
    int x = 0;
    int y = 0;
    cout << "Please enter a value for x: " ;
    cin << x;    // #1
    cin >> x;    // #2
    cin >> x     // #3
    cin x;       // #4
    cin >< x;    // #5
    x >> cin;    // #6
    return 0;
}
```

2. Must you always use `cin` with `cout`? Why or why not?

3. What is the redirect operator, and how is it used to process user input?

4. Can you use `cin` to store a value in a variable that already has a value?

5. Write code that allows the user to enter an integer value and store it in a variable. Your code should prompt the user, receive their input, and then print their input value back to them.

6. Add some functionality to the code you wrote for the previous exercise. Add two new variables, one `char` and one `float` or `double`. Prompt the user properly for each value. The program should print out the values of the variables, clearly labeled, on separate lines.

6.2   Review Answers

1. Only #2 (`cin >> x;`) is correct.

2. You do not need to to use `cin` statements exclusively with `cout` statements, though it is good practice to provide adequate feedback to users.

3. The redirect operator is >>, and it is used in conjunction with `cin` on the left and a variable on the right that receives the value entered by the user.

4. Yes, and the previous value is overwritten.

6.3   Further Reading

• http://www.cplusplus.com/reference/iolibrary

• http://www.cplusplus.com/doc/tutorial/basic_io

Chapter 7

Arithmetic

One of the most important things provided by C++ is the ability to do math. Everything a computer sees is a number. To a computer, its ability to do math and manipulate numbers is as essential to it as breathing is to us. (My apologies to anything not living that may be reading this).

The operators (+, -, *, /) in C++ are slightly different from what you may be used to from your second-grade math class. Addition is still a plus sign (+) and subtraction is still a minus sign (-). On the other hand, multiplication becomes an asterisk (*) and division becomes a forward slash (/). Think of the forward slash as *over* as in "5 over 9" is the same as the fraction $5/9$ or $\frac{5}{9}$.

To do math in C++, you will either want a variable to store the answer, or output the answer to the user.

The following code directly outputs the answer to the user:

```
cout << 9 + 2; // Prints 11
```

This code shows how to use a variable to store the answer:

```
int sum = 9 + 2; // sum now holds 11
```

Note that when you use a variable to store an answer, the variable must come first in the equation (before the equal sign) and must be the only thing on the left side of the equation. There are some other things to note. When you use more complicated equations, you can use parentheses to help. C++ uses a familiar order of operations (Parentheses, Exponents, Multiply, Divide, Add, and Subtract, or PEMDAS), but without the exponent operation (this topic is covered in Chapter 17). However, unlike in normal arithmetic, parentheses do not imply multiplication. For example, (4) (3), which we might expect to mean "4 times 3" does not mean the same as 4 * 3, the correct syntax. The expression (4) (3) results in a syntax error and will not compile. The compiler returns an error message like this:

    'error: '4' cannot be used as a function.'

In C++, there are several methods of shortening and simplifying the code you're creating. The first is the increment operator (++), which is found in the name of the language, C++. This operator increases the value of the variable it's applied to by 1. Conversely, the decrement (--) operator decreases the value by 1.

Keep in mind that order does matter with the increment and decrement operators. They can be used as either prefixes or suffixes, but where you put the operator results in slightly different behavior. Starting with similarities, C++ and ++C both increase value of C by one. The difference lies in when another variable is being set to that incremented value, such as B = C++. B will be set to C before C is incremented. B = ++C will cause B to be set to C+1, in a similar way to B = 1 + C.

```
int A;
A = 4;
A++;
//A contains 5
```

```
int A;
A = 9;
A--;
//A contains 8
```

```
int A, B;
B = 7;
A = B++;
//A contains 7, B contains 8
```

```
int A, B;
B = 7;
A = ++B;
//A contains 8, B contains 8
```

```
int A, B;
B = 3;
A = B--;
//A contains 3, B contains 2
```

Expression	Equivalent to
A *= 3;	A = A * 3;
B -= 5;	B = B - 5;
C /= 10;	C = C / 10;

Table 7.1: Examples of compound assignment updates

```
int A, B;
B = 3;
A = —B;
//A contains 2, B contains 2
```

Compound assignment operators can decrease the amount you type and can make your code more readable. These are the operators +=, -=, *=, and /=. What makes these operators special is that they use the value you want to change in the operation. For example, x += 2 is equivalent to x = x + 2.

Keep in mind the order that was used, as this becomes important with subtraction and division. The variable being changed is equivalent to the two leftmost variables in the longhand expression. Let's say we have X and Y, and want to set X equal to the value of Y divided by the value of X. This is impossible with this method, as X /= Y is equivalent to X = X / Y, and Y /= X is equivalent to Y = Y / X.

Here is some sample code using the concepts we presented in this chapter:

```cpp
#include <iostream>

using namespace std;

int main()
{
    int a = 5, b = 10, c = 15, d = 20;

    cout << "a + b = " << a + b << endl;
    cout << "d - c = " << d - c << endl;
    cout << "a * b = " << a * b << endl;
    cout << "d / a = " << d / a << endl;
}
```

The output of this code is:
```
a + b = 15
d - c = 5
a * b = 50
d / a = 4
```

7.1   Review Questions

1. Write a statement declaring two integer variables a and b and initialize them to 6 and 3, respectively.

2. Without changing the last line, fix the following code so there will be an output of 12.

```
int a = 4, b= 2;
a = a + 2 * b;
cout << a;
```

3. What is the output of the following code?

```
int a = 2, b = 5, c = 6;
a++;
b = b * a;
c = (c - a) + 3;
cout << a << endl;
cout << b << endl;
cout << c << endl;
```

4. What is the output of the following code?

```
int a, b, c;
a = 2;
b = 8;
c = 1;
c = b - b;
c = a + a;
c = b * 8;
b = b + b;
c = a + c;
b = a + b;
a = a * c;
b = a - c;
c = b + a;
cout << a << endl;
cout << b << endl;
cout << c << endl;
```

5. What is the output of the following code?

```
int a = 4, b = 2, c, d;
a = b + 3;
b++;
c = (b + 4) * 2;
c = c + 2;
d = a + b - 3;
a++;
a = a + 2 - b;
b = b * 2;
cout << "a=" << a << endl;
cout << "b=" << b << endl;
cout << "c=" << c << endl;
cout << "d=" << d << endl;
```

6. What is the output of the following code?

```
int m = 3, n = 2, x, y;
x = m + 5;
m--;
y = (m + 4) / 3;
n = n + 2;
m = m + n / 2;
m++;
x = x * 2 - 3;
y = y * 2;
n = n + y * 3
cout << "m=" << m << endl;
cout << "n=" << n << endl;
cout << "x=" << x << endl;
cout << "y=" << y << endl;
```

7.2   Review Answers

1. `int a = 6, b = 3;`

2.
```
int a = 4, b = 2;
a = (a + 2) * b;
cout << a;
```

3. 3

   15

   5

4. 132

   66

   198

5. a=5

   b=6

   c=16

   d=5

6. m=5

   n=16

   x=13

   y=4

7.3 Further Reading

- http://www.cplusplus.com/doc/tutorial/operators/
- http://www.sparknotes.com/cs/c-plus-plus-fundamentals/basiccommands/section1.rhtml

Chapter 8

Comments

As a C++ programmer, comments will make your life easier. They are meant to serve as notes, not just for you, but for anyone that may attempt to read your code. To this end, comments are a quick explanation of the code. There are two kinds of comments, **single-line comments** and **multi-line comments**.

Single-line comments typically come after a line of code. For a single-line comment, simply type a double slash // at the end of the line, and follow it with whatever notes you like, preferably to explain what that line of code does. Alternatively, the comment can start on a line of its own. Here are some examples:

```
int count; // This variable was declared
           // to count something
count = count + 1; // Increments count by 1

// Variable declared, and initialized to pi
float length = 3.14159;
```

Multi-line comments, sometimes called **block comments**, are used when you have a lot to say. They begin with a slash star (/*) and are ended by a star slash (*/). Here is an example:

```
/*
 * This is a
 * multi-line
 * comment
 */

/* This is also a comment */
```

Block comments do not need a star at the beginning of every line (as in the preceding example), but many programmers write it anyways, because it makes it easier to see and understand that "this is still a comment, don't write code here." Some development environments will automatically color-code certain pieces of code, so comments might be gray, for example, and the * at the beginning of each line might be unnecessary in that case. However, someone else may use a different development environment that does not use colors, so the stars can still improve readability.

Keep in mind when commenting, the point is to be clear and concise. Try to explain what's happening as accurately as possible, but try to keep it short. As you learn C++, use comments to explain what you're doing and why. You have to assume that the person reading your code needs an explanation for each non-trivial line.

```
//Commenting at the beginning of the file
//Allows you to give a summary of your program
#include <iostream>
using namespace std;

int main()
{
    // This cout statement outputs to the screen
    cout << "Hello world" << endl;
    cout << "What's the date?" << endl;

    // Comments should be used to explain things that may
    // not be obvious to someone other than you
    cin >> date; // Takes the date from the user

    /*
     * You can also use comments to remind yourself of
     * changes you want to make, e.g.
     * "debug code past this point"
     */
    return 0;
}
```

8.1 Review Questions

1. Comment each line of this code:

```
#include <iostream>

using namespace std;

int main()
{
    int time;
    cout << "Enter time \n";
    cin >> time;
    int answer = (32 * time * time) / 2;
    cout << "The distance is ";
    cout << answer;
    cout << " seconds \n";
    return 0;
}
```

2. Fix this code by removing or modifying comments so that it runs and compiles as it should.

```
/* #include <iostream> includes the iostream *

using namespace std;

int main()
{
    int time;                           // A place to store the time
    cout << "Enter time \n";  // Ask to enter the time
    cin >> time;                        // Takes user input
    int answer = (32 * time * time) / 2; // Calculates it
    cout << "The distance is ";         /* Outputs
    cout << answer;                         the distance
    cout << " seconds \n";                  in seconds */
    return 0;
}
```

3. Explain the purpose of commenting. How does it help you? Why would someone else need to be able to understand your code?

4. Write and properly comment your own simple program.

5. Go back to the program you wrote from the previous question. Add further comments that explain what's happening and share the commented code

with a classmate or friend. Ask them if they understand what's happening from just the comments.

6. Add comments to the following code.

   Note: Save percentages in hockey are shown to three decimal places and not multiplied by 100: .900 instead of 90%.

```cpp
#include <iostream>
#include <cstdlib>
using namespace std;
int main()
{
  double shots, goals, saves, save_perc;
  char cont;

  do {
    cout.unsetf(ios::fixed);
    cout.unsetf(ios::showpoint);

    cout << "Enter the number of shots on goal:\t";
    cin >> shots;
    cout << "Enter the number of goals scored:\t";
    cin >> goals;
    cout << endl;

    saves = shots - goals;
    save_perc = (saves / shots);

    cout << "If there were " << shots << " shots and "
      << goals << " goals\n";
    cout << "then the goalie's save percentage was ";

    cout.setf(ios::fixed);
    cout.setf(ios::showpoint);
    cout.precision(3);

    cout << save_perc << endl << endl;

    cout << "Run again? Y/N\t";
    cin >> cont;
    cont = toupper(cont);
  } while (cont == 'Y');
  return 0;
}
```

8.2 Review Answers

1. Answers will vary

2.
```cpp
#include <iostream> /* includes the iostream */

using namespace std;

int main()
{
    int time;                   // A place to store the time
    cout << "Enter time \n";    // Ask to enter the time
    cin >> time;                // Takes user input
    int answer = (32 * time * time) / 2; // Calculates it
    cout << "The distance is ";          // Outputs
    cout << answer;                      // the distance
    cout << " seconds\n";                // in seconds
    return 0;
}
```

3. Comments help you check that you know what you're doing and make sure you are doing everything that needs to be done. They also help other people understand your code, which is especially useful if your logic is different from theirs.

4. Answers will vary.

5. Keep trying until someone else understands the code from the comments alone.

6. Answers will vary.

Chapter 9

Data Types and Conversion

Suppose you need to carry two products across a farmyard: apples and water. The container you choose would depend on the product, and how much of the product you have to move. You might choose a small hand basket to carry a few apples, and a larger bushel basket to carry a large number of apples. Similarly, you could use a one-gallon bucket or a five-gallon bucket, depending on how much water you expected to move.

In a similar way, we choose data types to describe the type of data we would like to store in a variable, and "how much" of that data we expect to store.

Every variable has a **data type** which describes the range of possible values that may be stored in the variable. The C++ language defines a handful of basic types, some of which were discussed in Chapter 4. These types, their sizes (which may vary depending on the operating system), and the range of possible values can be found in Table 9.1. Additionally, the C++11 standard provides for the `long long int` data type as described in Table 9.2.

Several of the integer types have unsigned versions, which may only contain values greater than or equal to zero. The **floating-point types** do not have unsigned versions, as the sign is part of the standard that defines how these variables are represented in memory.

`bool`	1 byte	`true` or `false`
`char`	1 byte	-128 to 127
`short int` (`short`)	2 bytes	$-32,768$ to $32,767$
`int`	4 bytes	$-2,147,483,648$ to $2,147,483,647$
`long int` (`long`)	4 bytes	$-2,147,483,648$ to $2,147,483,647$
`float`	4 bytes	See "Floating-point Types" below
`double`	8 bytes	See "Floating-point Types" below
`long double`	8 bytes[1]	See "Floating-point Types" below

Table 9.1: Common data types and their ranges of values

Type	Size	Range of Values
`long long int` (`long long`)	8 bytes	$-9,223,372,036,854,775,808$ to $9,223,372,036,854,775,807$

Table 9.2: C++11's `long long int` data type

9.1   Floating-point types

Floating-point types are used to represent numbers that are not whole integers. For example:

```
float f = 3.35;
```

Variables of type `float` and of type `double` store these numbers in similar components as scientific notation, so the above value could be represented as 335×10^{-2}. The first part, 335, (sometimes called the **coefficient** or **significand**) is stored separately from the second part, -2, (called the **exponent**). The types can represent

---

[1]A `long double` *might* be stored as an 80-bit extended precision type, but this is dependent on the compiler. Variables of this type will be at least as large as a `double`.

Type	Size	Range of Values
unsigned char	1 byte	0 to 255
unsigned short	2 bytes	0 to 65, 535
unsigned int	4 bytes	0 to 4, 294, 967, 295
unsigned long	4 bytes	0 to 4, 294, 967, 295
unsigned long long[2]	8 bytes	0 to 18, 446, 744, 073, 709, 551, 615

Table 9.3: Unsigned types

Type	Exponent Range	Significand Range
float	0 to 255	2^{23}: 8, 388, 608 possible values
double	0 to 2, 048	2^{52}: 4, 503, 599, 627, 370, 496 possible values
long double	0 to 2, 048	2^{52}: 4, 503, 599, 627, 370, 496 possible values

Table 9.4: Floating point types

different ranges of significand and exponents, as shown in Table 9.4.

In fact, we can use scientific notation in conjunction with floating-point variables. The previous code that assigned a value to f can also be written as:

```
float f = 335e-2; // Sets f to 3.35
```

Both float and double include a few special values that represent nonnumeric results, such as infinity, negative infinity, and NaN (Not a Number).

```
float g = 10.0 / 0.0; // g is set to infinity
float h = g * -1.0;    // h is set to negative infinity
float i = g / h;
// Since infinity divided by negative infinity is
// undefined, the result of the division is not a
// number, and i is set to NaN
```

---

[2]This data type is found in the C++11 standard.

9.2   Other types introduced by C++11

C++11 provides the `cstdint` library, which defines several additional types that may be convenient. These types are listed in Table 9.5.

Type	Purpose	Unsigned version
`intmax_t`	The integer of maximum size supported on the platform	`uintmax_t`
`int8_t`	An integer of exactly 8 bits	`uint8_t`
`int16_t`	An integer of exactly 16 bits	`uint16_t`
`int32_t`	An integer of exactly 32 bits	`uint32_t`
`int64_t`	An integer of exactly 64 bits	`uint64_t`

Table 9.5: Data types found in C++11's `cstdint` library

These types are provided in part because the basic types like `int` and `short` are not guaranteed to be of any particular size, which can cause problems when compiling the same code on different platforms.

9.3   Conversion Between Types

It is sometimes necessary to convert a variable of one type to another, perhaps in order to pass the variable to a function that doesn't support the variable's original type. Here is an example of a variable of type `int` being converted (automatically) to a `double`:

```
int x = 2;
double y;
y = x; // Type conversion: the integer 2 is converted
       // to the double 2.0
cout << "y = " << y << endl; // This prints y = 2
```

This example demonstrates a **widening conversion**, since any possible value of x can be represented in y. On the other hand, we can do the reverse conversion:

```
int x;
double y = 2.0;
x = y; // Type conversion: the double 2.0 is converted
       // to the int 2
cout << "x = " << x << endl; // This prints x = 2
```

This code compiles and runs, but the compiler produces the following warning:
`warning: converting to 'int' from 'double'`

The compiler has a good reason for this warning: not all possible values that can be represented in a `double` can be represented in an `int`. We refer to this as a **narrowing conversion**. If we change the code slightly, we can see where problems can occur:

```
int x;
double y = 2.9;
x = y; // Type conversion: the double 2.9 is converted
       // to the int 2
cout << "x = " << x << endl; // This prints x = 2
```

Because integers cannot represent the numbers after the decimal point, they are simply dropped. This might seem counterintuitive, as we might expect the values to be rounded up from 2.9 to 3. Fortunately, C++11 provides a `round()` function in the <`cmath`> library that returns the integer closest to the passed parameter:

```
int x;
double y = 2.9;
x = round(y);
// round(y) returns the double 3.0 (the closest integer
// to the passed parameter) This double is then
// converted to the int 3
cout << "x = " << x << endl; // This prints x = 2
```

9.4 Coercion & Casting

The examples in the previous section relied on the compiler to perform the conversions from `int` to `double` and `double` to `int`. This implicit, automatic conversion is often referred to as **coercion**, and can be found in the following example:

```
int z = 3.3 + 4.8; // z is set to the integer 8
                   // (coerced from the double 8.1)
```

The compiler still warns us that it is converting the `double` to an `int`. In this case, we know that we want an integer value, so we can tell the compiler to explicitly convert the `double`s to `int`s using explicit **casts**, as follows:

```
int z = (int)3.3 + (int)4.8; // z is set to 7
```

We enclose the "target" type in parentheses (in this case, `int`) and place it before the value or expression we want to convert. Doing this removes the warning that the compiler produces when it coerces the double to int. The above still isn't quite what we want, though, since the individual doubles are converted to 3 and 4, respectively. (Remember that converting from a double to an int drops the part after the decimal point rather than rounding!) It would be better to convert the result of the addition, rather than the individual values, like this:

```
int z = (int)(3.3 + 4.8);  // z is set to 8
```

9.5   Automatic Types in C++11

C++11 introduces the auto data type, which leaves the determination of a variable's type up to the compiler. At compile time, the data type of the value that is assigned determines the data type that replaces the auto type. Some of the syntax in the second line below may be unfamiliar—for a description of what's happening there, refer to Chapter 19.

```
auto myVar = 3;         // myVar is an int
auto myVar2 = &myVar;   // myVar2 is an int*
auto myVar3 = 't';      // myVar3 is a char
```

The decltype operator is another new feature, which extracts types from objects and is used in a similar way as auto:

```
auto myVar = 3;                // myVar is an int
decltype(myVar) myVar4;        // myVar4 is an int
decltype(myVar < 1) myVar5;    // myVar5 is a bool
```

In these examples, it is easy to determine the types assigned to the variable, but the power of auto is in conjunction with complicated types like iterators of container objects as discussed more in Chapter 23. Here is an example:

```
std::vector<int> v;  // Create a vector of integers
v.push_back(2);  // Add an element containing 2 to the vector
v.push_back(8);  // Add an element containing 8 to the vector
auto myIterator = v.begin();
// The above is equivalent to:
// std::vector<int>::iterator myIterator = v.begin();
```

9.6   Review Questions

1. What's the difference between the various data types that store numbers? Why would you use one over the other?

2. If you assign the result of an `int` divided by an `int` to a `float` (e.g. `float num = 13/7;`), what could happen to the resulting value?

3. Declare a variable named `sampleSize` and set it to 14.58093.

4. Write code that increases `sampleSize` by 12.495.

9.7   Review Answers

1. `int`s only store whole numbers. `float`s and `double`s can store numbers with decimal points. `int`s are useful for anything that cannot have fractional parts, and you might also use a `double` for very large numbers.

2. The fractional part is left off. (`num` is 1 in the example)

3. `double sampleSize = 14.58093;`

4. `sampleSize += 12.495;`

9.8   Further Reading

- http://www.cplusplus.com/reference/cstdint/
- http://en.wikipedia.org/wiki/Floating_point
- http://en.wikipedia.org/wiki/IEEE_floating_point
- http://learncpp.com/cpp-tutorial/25-floating-point-numbers/

Chapter 10

Conditionals

Conditionals are used to direct the program to different sections of code. In plain English, we might have a statement "If X is greater than Y, do this..." Conditionals direct the program to behave differently depending on the results of a comparison. Several common comparison operators used in C++ are:

Symbol	Meaning
==	Is equal to
!=	Is not equal to
>=	Greater than or equal to
<=	Less than or equal to
>	Greater than
<	Less than
&&, and	Logical AND: The condition on the left *AND* the condition on the right must be true
||, or	Logical OR: The condition on the left *OR* the condition on the right must be true

Table 10.1: Common comparison operators

10.1 `if`, `else`, and `else if`

The most popular conditional is the `if` statement. An `if` statement looks like this:

```
if ( variable == variable2 )
{
    // Code here executes only when
    // the value of variable is the same as variable2
}
```

The keyword `if` is used to start the statement. Parentheses are used to contain the conditional expression. If the expression inside the parentheses is true, then the following expression will be executed.

10.1.1 A small digression on expressions

Note that curly braces merely surround expressions to become a single expression. The act of surrounding expressions creates a code block. However, having only one expression within a code block is the same as not having it in a code block.

```
if (variable == variable2 )
{
    cout << "Yes!";
}
```

is the same as

```
if (variable == variable2 )
    cout << "Yes!";
```

It is not recommended to go without braces for mere brevity at the cost of making mistakes later on. For example, suppose you have some code for baking bread, like the following.

```
if (breadType == 10)
    ovenFanOn = true;
```

Then later you are told that bread type 10 needs to be cooked at 350 °F. So you make the following change:

```
if (breadType == 10)
    ovenFanOn = true;
    ovenTemp = 350;
```

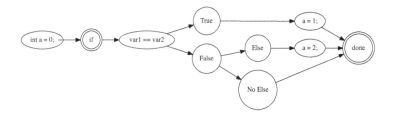

Figure 10.1: `if` and `else` statement flow of execution

Except that is really the same as:

```
if (breadType == 10)
   ovenFanOn = true;

ovenTemp = 350;
```

Now the baker is upset because every loaf is being cooked wrong except bread of type 10! What you really meant was:

```
if (breadType == 10)
{
   ovenFanOn = true;
   ovenTemp = 350;
}
```

Here's another bear trap that you'll likely hit:

```
if (breadType == 9);
   ovenFanOn = true;
```

It is still valid syntax, but the expression after the `if` statement is an empty expression. An empty expression does nothing, and so now every bread type will have the fan on, which is not what the baker wanted.

10.1.2 Using `else`

An `else` statement may be placed after an `if` statement, and any time the expression inside the parentheses following the `if` is not true, the code inside the `else` block is executed. For example:

```
int a = 0;
if(var1 == var2)
{
   // Code here executes only when
   // the value of variable is the same as variable2
   a = 1;
}
else
{
   // Code here executes if they are not the same
   a = 2;
}
```

An else statement is used when you want some code to execute in any other case where the if statement is not true. An example of how this works is also shown in Figure 10.1.

An else if could also be placed after the if statement. An else if is an additional if statement checked only when the previous if statement is false. While else is a catch-all, else if chains an if to test for other conditions. Multiple else if statements can be used, and they are all checked sequentially, and if necessary, an else statement can be included at the end as a final catch-all. Take a look at Figure 10.2 for a flowchart example.

Here's what the three statements would look like all together:

```
if(a == b)
{
   cout << "They are the same!" << endl;
}
else if(a > b)
{
   cout << "a is bigger!" << endl;
}
else
{
   cout << "a is smaller!" << endl;
}
```

Note that every conditional expression is in parentheses. Each if must be followed by a (. . .) (with a Boolean expression inside the parentheses) in C++. Conditional expressions also appear in loops (discussed in Chapter 12) and switch statements.

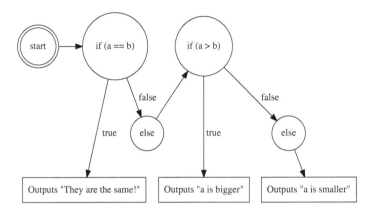

Figure 10.2: How `if-else` chaining works

10.2 `switch` statements

`switch` statements (also sometimes called `switch-case` statements) make a menu-like set of blocks. It does the same job as many `if` statements, but can simplify the job when used correctly. Here is an example:

```
switch(variable)
{
  case 1:
    //code to execute when variable is equal to 1
    break;
  case 2:
    //code to execute when variable is equal to 2
    break;
  default:
    //code to execute when variable is neither 1 nor 2
    break;
}
// Resume here after a break
```

If `variable` is equal to 1 then the code following `case 1:` will be executed. If it is equal to 2, then the code following `case 2:` will be executed, and if it is

equal to neither, then the code following `default:` will be executed. The cases
are separated by the `break` statement, which forces the code to leave the `switch`
statement's block of code. This code:

```
switch(variable)
{
  case  1:
    cout << "You picked case 1. Lame.";
    break;

  case  2:
    cout << "Case two is way better.";
    break;

  default:
    cout << "WRONG!";
    break;
}
```

is equivalent to this code:

```
if (variable == 1)
{
  cout <<  "You picked case 1. Lame.";
}
else if (variable == 2)
{
  cout << "Case two is way better.";
}
else
{
  cout << "WRONG!";
}
```

When there are only a few cases, `if`, `else if`, and `else` statements are
often easier. However, when you get to a greater number of cases, `switch` statements become easier.

In `switch` statements, only one `case`'s code executes, provided that each
`case` is followed by `break`. Otherwise, the program continues execution until
it reaches a `break` statement or the end of the `switch` block. With an `if` and
`else if`, only one branch may be executed, and the condition in the `else if`
is only evaluated if the condition in the `if` is `false`.

Here is some code that uses both `switch` and `if` statements. Compiling and
running the following code results in the output in Table 10.2.

User enters	Output
`//Program start`	<1> Addition
	<2> Subtraction
	<3> Compare
	Type the number of your desired option:
1	The result of this addition is 9.3
2	The result of this subtraction is 0.9
3	A is greater than B
`//anything other than 1, 2, or 3`	Not an option

Table 10.2: The sample program's output

```
#include <iostream>
using namespace std;
int main() {
    int choice;
    double a = 5.1, b = 4.2;

    cout << "<1> Addition\n<2> Subtraction\n<3> Compare\n";
    cout << "Type the number of your desired option:\t";
    cin >> choice;

    switch(choice) {
      case 1:
        cout << "The result of this addition is "
          << a + b << endl << endl;
        break;
      case 2:
        cout << "The result of this subtraction is "
          << a - b << endl << endl;
        break;
      case 3:
        if (a > b)
          cout << "A is greater than B";
        else if (a < b)
          cout << "A is less than B";
        else //a == b
          cout << "A equals B";
        break;
      default:
        cout << "Not an option";
        break;
    }
    return 0;
}
```

10.3 Review Questions

1. What is the output of the following code?

```
int a = 5;
int b = 10;

if (a > b)
    cout << "a is greater than b.";
else
    cout << "b is greater than a.";
```

2. Why are switch statements useful?

3. When are braces ({}) needed in an if statement?

4. Write a program that checks which number is higher than another and prints out an appropriate message. This program should use 2 variables, an if statement and an else statement. Bonus: Rewrite it to also check if the numbers are equal.

10.4 Review Answers

1. b is greater than a.

2. switch statements are useful for making menus for the user. (Other answers are also possible)

3. Braces are needed for any code longer than 2 lines following an if.

4.
```
#include <iostream>
using namespace std;
int main()
{
    int input1, input2;
    cout << "enter a number: ";
    cin >> input1;
    cout << "enter a number to compare to the first: ";
    cin >> input2;
    if (input1 > input2)
        cout << input1 << " is greater than " << input2;
    else
        cout << input2 << " is greater than " << input1;
}
```

Chapter 11

Strings

Let's discuss **strings**. A `string` is a data type typically used to hold a collection of printable characters such as words, sentences, or longer sequences. In order to use strings in your program you must first include the string library:

```
#include <string>
using namespace std;
```

Also note that a `string`, for convenience, can be treated like an array of individual characters.

When we declare variables of type `string`, we declare them just like we would an `int`, `float`, or `double`. We can create a variable named `myString` of type string by doing this:

```
#include <string>
using namespace std;

string myString;
```

If you choose not to have `using namespace std;` in your code, the variable `myString` must be declared as follows:

```
#include <string>

std::string myString;
```

We can then store anything we want in that `string` as long as it is made up of characters. When a literal value is assigned to a `string`, it should be surrounded by double quotes such as in the case of `"Hello"`:

```
#include <string>

string myString = "Hello";
```

If we are storing the value of a `string` entered by a user, the user does not have to use quotes. We can store `"Hello"` in the `string` by doing the following:

```
string myString;
cin >> myString;  // User types: Hello
                  // myString is now "Hello"
```

It is also possible to use the arithmetic operator + with strings to concatenate (combine) the two strings. If we combined one `string` that contained `"Hello"` and another `string` that contained `"World"` the connected string would then read `"HelloWorld"`.

```
string v1 = "Hello",
       v2 = "World";
cout << v1 + v2 << endl;
// Outputs:
// HelloWorld
```

In order to have a space between the two words, one of the strings would need to contain a space such as this:

```
string v1 = "Hello", v2 = " World";
//                          ^
cout << v1 + v2 << endl;
// Outputs:
// Hello World
```

Or it can be represented as:

```
string v1 = "Hello ", v2 = "World";
//                 ^
cout << v1 + v2 << endl;
// Outputs:
// Hello World
```

Alternatively, a space can be added like so:

```
string v1 = "Hello", v2 = "World";
cout << v1 + " " + v2 << endl;
//-----------^-------------------
// Outputs:
// Hello World
```

The first two concatenates the two strings to create one string that contains "Hello World", and the third concatenates three strings to produce the same result.

When reading strings from std::cin, the default behavior is to collect all characters until the first whitespace (a tab, space, or newline) character that it finds in the input. For example, if the user inputs "Hello World" in the following code, std::cin stops reading at the first whitespace, and thus the string would contain only "Hello". If we want to read the entire line of text, we need to use the getline() function, which reads until the first newline character. This is how you use the getline() function:

```
string myString;
getline(cin, myString);
```

This function call will take the entire line of input, including all whitespace characters, and store it in the variable myString.

We can also find out the length of the string by using the member function length() with any string object. For example, if we wanted to find the length of a string entered by a user and store it in a variable named stringLength, we might do this:

```
string myString;
int stringLength;
getline(cin, myString);
stringLength = myString.length();
cout << "The string you entered was "
     << stringLength
     << " characters long."
     << endl;
```

Aside from finding the length of a string, we can search for certain characters in the string by using the find() and rfind() member functions. For example, if we wanted to find a single space in a string variable named myString that contains "Hello World", we would do this:

```
string myString = "Hello World";
int spot = myString.find(" ");
```

myString

Figure 11.1: A string viewed as an array

This code results in the value 5 being stored in the variable named spot because the space character is stored at index 5 if you treat the string as an array, as shown in Figure 11.1.

Remember that we start at index 0, so even though the space is in the sixth position, it is at index 5 in the string. When a line of text is stored in a string, think of it as being stored in memory in an array of the same length as there are characters in the string. For example, the string "Hello World" can be contained in an array with 11 slots, therefore the space character would be found in myString[5]. The find() function can also search within a string from some arbitrary starting point, instead of from the beginning:

```
string myString = "Hello World";
int spot, spot2;
spot = myString.find(" "); // Found at index 5
// Starting from index 5, found at index 7
spot2 = myString.find("o", spot);
```

The second argument that is passed to the function (in this case, spot) is the index at which you want to start your search.

We can also use the rfind() function to find a character in reverse direction from the end of the string, or from some starting point, as above. If we wanted to find the single character string "o" *before* the space we might do something like this:

```
string myString = "Hello World";
int spot, spot2;
spot = myString.rfind(" "); // found at index 5
// starting from index 5, found at index 4
spot2 = myString.rfind("o", spot);
```

This function call to rfind() uses the arguments "o" and spot. This stores the position of the first "o" it comes across after going in reverse from the index stored in `spot` (which contains 5). The last line would be equivalent to:

```
// starting from index 5, found at index 4
spot2 = myString.rfind("o", 5);
```

Both of these function calls will start searching for the string `"o"` backwards from the same spot in the string, at index 5.

Sometimes the string you search for cannot be found, as in this example:

```
string myString = "Hello World";
int spot = myString.find("Q"); // No Q in this string!
```

In this case, the `find()` (or `rfind()`, for that matter) returns a special value named `string::npos`. When we use `find()` or `rfind()` and believe that they could fail, we should verify that the string was found, as below:

```
string userInput;
int spot;
cin >> userInput;
spot = userInput.find("Z");

if (spot == string::npos)
    cout << "There was no Z in what you typed!" << endl;
else
    cout << "The first Z was in position " << spot << endl;
```

11.1 Review Questions

1. Write code to declare a `string` and take input from a user.

2. Can a `string` be treated as a character array?

3. When do you use a `string`?

4. What is the `#include` needed to use `strings`?

5. What function do you have to use to take an input with a space?

6. Write code that takes in 5 words and outputs each of them 4 times.

7. Write a program that takes in an input of at least two words of the same length. The program should then switch the last word and the first word.

11.2   Review Answers

1.
```
string myString;
cout << "Please input a string: ";
getline(cin, myString);
//cin >> myString; is also acceptable
```

2. Yes

3. When you need to hold a collection of printable characters such as words, sentences, or longer sequences.

4. `#include <string>`

5. `getline`

6.
```
string myString;
cout << "Please input a string: ";
getline(cin, myString);
//cin >> myString; is also acceptable
```

11.3   Further Reading

- http://www.harding.edu/fmccown/cpp_strings.pdf
- http://www.stanford.edu/class/cs106x/handouts/08-C++-Strings.pdf

Chapter 12

Loops

12.1 Introduction

Okay, so you know how to do some programming, but now you need to be able to handle a dozen or more operations that are obnoxiously repetitive. Imagine that you have a program that needs to allow data to be entered about your employees. Do you really want to have to write out the code to do that for every single individual? No—you want to set it up so you write it out as concisely as possible, and copy and paste just won't work. What we need to do is write the relevant code once and have it repeated for us as many times as necessary.

For this, we'll use a structure known as a **loop**, which does exactly what you expect it would. A loop allows you to repeat a section of code as many times as you need. When the code reaches the end of the section, it goes back to the top of the section and the loop starts again. After each repetition of the loop (which we call an **iteration**), it will check for an **end condition** that is specified by the programmer.

12.2 Having Fun `while` Programming

The first loop we'll cover is the `while` loop, probably the simplest and easiest-to-use loop. It's referred to as a **pretest loop** as it's designed to check the loop's end condition prior to a repetition of the loop.

In Figure 12.1, the basic model of a **pretest loop** is shown. A diamond is used to represent where a decision must be made. In this case, it's a Boolean expression. If the expression is true, control passes to the rectangle, which represents an action (or actions) to be performed: the statements that represent the body of the loop.

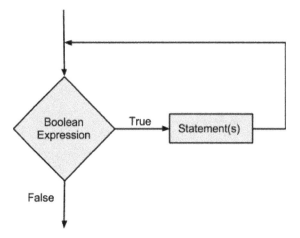

Figure 12.1: Logic of a while loop

As with everything else we've learned so far, syntax is important. The structure is simple enough, as the pseudocode below shows:

```
while (BooleanExpression)
{
  statement;
  statement;
  // whatever else needs to be done
}
```

The important thing to remember here is to be sure you have some statement to eventually allow the loop to exit. When the Boolean expression is false, remember, the loop is finished.

Also, note that, like an if statement, the braces are not necessary if there is only one statement following the line with the while keyword and Boolean expression. Is it recommended to use the braces with only one statement? For your own sanity, and that of others reading your code, yes. Do you have to? No, but some organizations' coding standards might say otherwise, because it makes the code easier to read and edit. So remember, it's best to start with good habits early.

Let's look at an actual example of a `while` loop.

```
int i = 10; // initializes i at 10

cout << "T-minus ";
// while loop that is ended when i is less than 0
while ( i >=0)
{
   // outputs the value of i, then moves to a new line
   cout << i << endl;
   // decreases the value of i by 1
   i--;
};

cout << "Lift Off!";
```

The above code prints a countdown:
10
9
8
7
6
5
4
3
2
1
Lift Off!

12.3 **do-while** Loops

Remember how the `while` loop is known as a pretest loop? Well, a do-while loop is known as a **post-test loop** for a similar reason. Let's take a look at the flowchart in Figure 12.2 and take a guess as to why.

Post-test loops perform the statements in the body of the loop *before* it tests the end condition. Let's look at how this will affect the syntax you will use when implementing the loop.

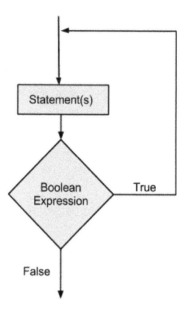

Figure 12.2: Logic of a do-while loop

```
do
{
    something;
    something;
    // whatever else needs to be done
} while (BooleanExpression)
```

The difference between a while and a do-while loop is where each checks its end condition. In this case, the line with the while and the end condition are after the main section of code. In a normal while loop, the program can potentially meet the end condition before even entering the loop body, and just pass over it. In a do-while loop, the program checks the end condition after each iteration of the loop, so it will run at least once before the loop ends.

There's not a whole lot more to add then hasn't been stated in the while loop section, so here's an example.

```
char cont;  // Short for continue;
            // continue is a key word and can't be used

do {
   cout << "Go Cadets!\n";
   cout << "Do you want to continue? Type Y for yes: \t";
   cin >> cont;
} while (cont == 'Y');
```

12.4   Event-Based Loops vs Count-Based Loops

Loops can be organized into two categories based on how you use them. These two categories are defined by if you want to do a certain number of iterations of the loop (a **count-controlled** loop) or continue until some event occurs, such as a particular user input (an **event-controlled** loop). Let's look at code examples to differentiate the two. The first example shows an event-controlled while loop.

```
// Declares sum and temp. Initializes sum to 0.
int sum=0, temp;

cout << "Please give a number to add: ";
// User inputs into a temporary variable to add to sum
cin >> temp;

while (temp != 0)
{
   // Sets sum equal to sum+temp at start of loop
   sum += temp;
   cout << endl << "total: " << sum << endl;
   //asks user to input temp variable again
   cout << "Add another number? If yes, input "
      << "a nonzero integer. If no, input 0." << endl;
   cin >> temp;
}
```

This example shows a count-controlled while loop:

```
int counter = 1;

while(counter != 12)
{
   cout << counter << endl;
   counter++;
}
```

12.5   **for** work or **for** play

Consider what we have needed for each loop we've covered. We've needed to initialize a variable that we want to check. We've also needed an end condition to test that variable against. Finally, we needed a way of modifying that variable to meet that end condition. After that, it's whatever we've felt like putting in. With the for loop, we put those three elements into the loop header, separated by semicolons (;). A for loop would would look something like this:

```
for(Intialization; Test; Update)
{
    something;
    something;
    // whatever else you need
}
```

The for loop by its nature lends itself to being a count-controlled loop. You use this kind of loop to count up (or down) each iteration until you get to the specified value.

Let's run through how a for loop should run, following the code below. Assuming everything is correct, you would initialize the first value to something such as an int counter that is set to 1. The TestExpression will include the same Boolean logic you would use in while and do-while loops, so let's just say when counter is less than or equal to 5, the loop will terminate. Finally, let's say counter++ is the update expression. In each iteration (unless you also decide to change counter from the body of the loop) you will move through this pretest loop four times.

This code corresponds to the logic in Figure 12.3:

```
for(int counter = 1; counter <= 5; counter++)
{
    cout << counter << endl;
}
```

...which produces the following output:

1
2
3
4
5

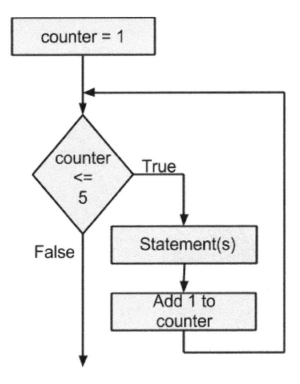

Figure 12.3: Logic of a for loop

12.6   Picking a Loop

Which loop you use is dependent on your preferences and needs. A for loop is nice, but it's more convenient as a count-controlled loop. If you needed to use an event-controlled loop, you may prefer to use a while or do-while loop. A for loop is a nice way to condense the initialization, end conditions and update statement of the loop into one short line. When choosing between a do-while and a while loop, you should remember that with a do-while, it will always run at least once, while a while loop may run zero or more times.

12.7   Nested Loops

Much like if statements, loops can be nested within each other. Just remember to practice good formatting habits to keep the code from being too confusing. Take a look at the example below, then let's talk our way through it.

```
//a single day
for(int hours = 0; hours < 24; hours++)
{
  // a single hour
  for(int minutes = 0; i < 60; minutes++)
  {
    //a single minute
    for(int seconds = 0; seconds < 60; seconds++)
    {
      //outputs the current time
      cout << hours << ":" << minutes
          << ":" << seconds << endl;
    }
  }
}
```

For those readers who concluded that this is a clock simulation, you are correct! Our system of time is set up that we have 24 hours in a day, and each hour is a 60 minute cycle, and each minute is a 60 second cycle. The code mimics this by advancing the seconds 60 times before advancing each minute. After 60 minutes, the hour counter loop is incremented. Each time an outer loop starts another iteration, variables inside the inner loops are reset.

12.8   Infinite Loops

Remember to have some way of advancing towards the end condition. What will happen if you can't reach that end condition from within the loop? Most likely an infinite loop will occur, which is a loop that can't stop itself. Depending on the operation of the loop, you may not know what is happening, and the loop could potentially cause disastrous results. Let's look at an example of a while loop that suffers from an infinite loop.

```
int counter = 1;

while(counter != 12)
{
  cout << counter << endl;
  counter += 2;
}
```

Because counter starts with a value of 1, and adds 2 each time the loop executes, counter will always be odd, and never equal twelve. Therefore, the loop will never end.

12.9 Review Questions

1. Create a while loop that increments some integer variable x initialized with a value of 0 by 3 until the value of x reaches a value of 30. Make sure you declare the variable and initialize it first!

2. Create a do-while loop that reads integer values given by the user into an integer variable x, initialized to 0, then adds those values onto some variable named totalVal until totalVal reaches at least 20.

3. Create a for loop that outputs your name to the screen 10 times before exiting the loop.

4. Spot the logic error and correct it in the following code:

```
for(int j = 10, j > 0, j--)
{
  cout << j << endl;
  if (j = 1)
  {
    cout << "BOOM!\n";
  }
}
```

5. In the last question, was the loop an event-controlled loop or count-controlled loop?

12.10 Review Answers

1.
```
int x = 0;
while (x < 10)
{
   x++;
}
```

2.
```
int x = 0;
int totalVal = 0;
do
{
   cout << "Type in a number: ";
   cin >> x;
   totalVal += x;
}
while (totalVal < 20);
```

3.
```
for(int i = 0; i < 10; i++)
{
   cout << "Your name here\n";
}
```

4.
```
for (int j = 10; j > 0; j--)
{
   cout << j << endl;
   if (j == 1)
   {
      cout << "BOOM!\n";
   }
}
```

5. Count-controlled

12.11 Further Reading

- http://www.cplusplus.com/doc/tutorial/control/
- http://www.cprogramming.com/tutorial/lesson3.html
- http://www.cprogramming.com/c++11/c++11-ranged-for-loop.html

Chapter 13

Arrays

An array is a series of variables that are the same of the same type (int, float, double, char, and so on). Arrays are held in a computer's memory in a strict linear sequence. An array does not hold anything other than the elements of the specified type, so there is no assigning an array of type float and hoping to store a string there. Doing so would cause a "type mismatch error" and the program wouldn't compile. To create an array, the programmer types something like this:

```
char  Scott[5];
```

The char is the data type for all elements in the array, Scott is the name of the array (you can be as creative as you want with the name), and the 5 inside the square brackets represents the size of the array. So char Scott[5] can hold 5 pieces of data that are of type char.

When trying to visualize an array, think of a rectangle split up into as many pieces as the array has places to hold data. In Figure 13.1, the rectangle has five spaces, each of type char awaiting some values.

In order to refer to the individual elements in an array, we start with the number 0 and count upwards. We use [0] to access the first element in the array, [1] for the second, [2] for the third, and so on. In order to read or write certain locations of the array, we state the name of the array and the element we want to access. It should look like this:

```
Scott[3]  =  'Q';
cout  <<  Scott[3];
```

The diagram below depicts how the computer interprets this.

71

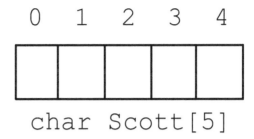

Figure 13.1: The array named Scott has five spaces for char data

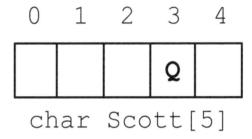

Figure 13.2: The fourth element of Scott now contains 'Q'

You can also store values inside the array ahead of time when you declare the array. To do so, you need to enclose the values of the appropriate type in brackets and separate the values with a comma. Below are two examples, one an array where each element is of type char and another where each element is of type int.

```
char Scott[5] = {'S', 'c', 'o', 't', 't'};
int John[5] = {99, 5, 1, 22, 7};
```

Note that, in the C and C++ language, arrays of characters intended to be treated as a string must contain a special character called the **null character**[1] or

---

[1]Often abbreviated NUL; Note that this is not the same as the NULL pointer

null terminator. The null terminator marks the end of the string. In C++, this is represented by the special character `'\0'`. Because the null temrinator takes up one element in the array, any character array that is intended to be used as a printable string must be declared having a size one larger than the longest string that you expect to store. Initializing the above character array should really be done as the following (notice that we make the array one element larger!):

```
char Scott[6] = { 'S', 'c', 'o', 't', 't', '\0' };
```

Alternatively, you can initialize a character array with a string literal, as below. We discuss string literals in more detail in Chapter 3.

```
char Scott[6] = "Scott";
```

It is also possible to let the computer figure out the appropriate length for an array when the array is being initialized at the same time as when it is declared. The below code produces an identical array as the previous example:

```
char Scott[] = "Scott";
```

13.1 Multi-dimensional Arrays

A two-dimensional array (some might call it a "matrix") is the same thing as an array, but is an "array of arrays". Here's a two-dimensional three-by-three array:

```
int Rich[3][3]; // 2D
```

Declaring arrays with more dimensions are possible with similar syntax. Here's a three-dimensional $10 \times 10 \times 10$ example:

```
int Sam[10][10][10]; // 3D
```

And here is a four-dimensional $10 \times 10 \times 10 \times 10$ array. This is possible even though it's hard to visualize.

```
int Travis[10][10][10][10]; // 4D
```

A user can input values into a multi-dimensional array in a similar way as a single-dimensional array.

---

described in Chapter 19.

```
int  neo[3][3]  =  {{1,2,3},  {4,5,6},  {7,8,9}};
cout  <<  neo[0][0]  <<  endl  <<  endl;  // first  number,  1
cout  <<  "  "  <<  neo[2][2];  // last  number,  9
```

The same logic is applied for 3-dimensional and 4-dimensional arrays, but when filling them be mindful of the order of the input so that when you want to view certain elements in the array you are able to correctly access them.

13.2   Review Questions

1. Declare an integer array named myInt with a size of 10.

2. If an array has a size of 20, how many indexes are there in the array and what are they?

3. Declare a character array named myArray with a size of 4, and initialize the characters in the array to 'Z', 'a', 'c', and 'h'.

4. Create a program in which an integer array named myArray is declared with a size of 10. Use a for loop to prompt the user to store a value in every index of the array. After the array is given values, output the values of the array to the screen using a for loop. Output each value of the array on its own line.

13.3   Review Answers

1. int myInt[10];

2. There are 20: indexes 0 through 19.

3. char myArray[4] = 'Z', 'a', 'c', 'h';

4.
```
#include <iostream>
using namespace std;
int main()
{
  int myArray[10];
  cout << "Enter 10 integers, press [ENTER] "
    << "after every integer.\n";
  for (int i = 0; i < 10; i++)
  {
    cin >> myArray[i];
  }
  for (int j = 0; j < 10; j++)
  {
    cout << myArray[j] << endl;
  }
  return 0;
}
```

13.4 Further Reading

- http://www.cplusplus.com/doc/tutorial/arrays/
- http://www.cplusplus.com/forum/beginner/43663/
- http://msdn.microsoft.com/en-us/library/7wkxxx2e.aspx
- https://www.youtube.com/watch?v=SFGOAKYXfOo

Chapter 14

Blocks, Functions, and Scope

14.1 Blocks

Since we've covered `if` statements and loops, let's go into more detail about the code that's contained within them. When you need to contain multiple lines of code, we've shown how to use braces. These braces will create a new layer in the code, and the lines within would be grouped into what is known as a compound statement, sometimes called a block.

Take a look at the example below. There are two blocks here: the one where x is less than 5, and one where x is greater than 5. Notice the variables declared in each, y and z. When these are declared, they are only usable within the blocks that they were declared. When that block reaches its end, they are lost to the rest of the program. This is because the scope of the variables within the blocks is limited to those blocks. We discuss scope further at the end of this chapter.

77

```cpp
int x;
cin << x;

if (x < 5)
{
    int y;      // Declares y
    cin << y;   // User input stored in y
    x += y;     // Sets y to x + y
}
else if (x > 5)
{
    int z;      // Declares z
    cin << z;   // User input stored in z
    x -= z;     // Sets x to x - z
}

cout >> x;
```

14.2   Basic Functions in C++

14.2.1   What are functions and why do we use them?

Functions are an important part of C++ programming. Without them, programs would be confusing and difficult to troubleshoot. When programs are written, they tend to be written in logical chunks which we call subprograms. These subprograms are known as functions in C++ which, when called in a program, may execute whatever the programmer wants. Simply put, functions are like miniature programs that when pieced together form the actual program that you are trying to write.

14.2.2   The parts of a basic function

A **function declaration** (sometimes known as the **prototype**) is normally placed before the main() function in your code. This lets the compiler know that there is a function that will be defined in more detail further on in your program. With basic functions, your declarations should start with a **return type** such as double, int, and so on; this is the data type your function will return.

After the return type, the next item that needs to be written is the function's name, which can be almost anything you want. Remember that you will be using it again later in your code, so it makes sense to make it something short and logical that you can remember! Now that you have your data type and your function name, it's time for zero or more function **parameters**. These will be written inside parentheses immediately following your function's name. Each parameter is in turn made

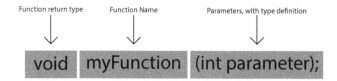

Figure 14.1: The structure of a function declaration

up of a data type and a name like a variable declaration. A comma separates function parameters and your declaration must end with a semicolon after the closing right parenthesis. Here is an example of a function declaration:

```
// cost and price are parameters
double profit (int cost, double price);
```

Using a function looks much like an abbreviated version of the function declaration. A **function call** is responsible for telling the compiler when and how to execute a function. Function calls are found in another function like main(). Often the user is prompted to enter necessary data with cout statements and his or her response is collected with cin. Once this data is collected, the program holds it until a function call is made somewhere in the code. Once the function call is made, the compiler takes the entered data and then uses the code in the **function definition** (which we will go over shortly) to operate on the parameters and return a value. For your function call, write your function name followed by the variables or values you want to pass in. In a functiton call, it is not necessary to specifty the data types, as they are already understood.

Here is an example of a function call:

```cpp
#include <iostream>
using namespace std;

// function declaration (prototype)
double profit (int cost, double price);

int main ()
{
  double a, b;
  int c;
  cout << "Enter the manufacturing cost of the item: ";
  cin >> c;
  cout << "Enter the retail price of the item: ";
  cin >> b;

  // function call to profit with cost = c and price = b
  a = profit (c, b);
  cout << a << endl;
  return 0;
}
```

You have a declaration and a function call now. The only thing left is the code inside the function definition—the **function body** is the most important part because it contains the code needed by the compiler to execute the function.

The function definition will usually have a lot more code than both the declaration and the function call. As a result, the definition and body are also more difficult to write than the declaration or call. The function definition and body is often placed after your main() function. Multiple function definitions and bodies can be placed after your main() in no particular order, though it makes it less confusing if you use the same order as when they were declared. Start your function definition with your **function heading**, which looks exactly like your function declaration but without a semicolon. Following your heading, you need your function body. Start your function body by placing an opening left brace ({) on the line following your heading. The code that makes up the function body follows the brace. After the code in the body is finished, you end the body with a closing right brace (}). Notice that the semicolon is not necessary either after your heading or after your closing brace. The standard rules for semicolons apply within the body of the function, though. What goes inside the function body depends completely on what you want the function to do. You may declare variables to be used just in your function and can leave the function using return statements at any time.

Below is an example of a function definition:

```
// function definition
double profit (int cost, double price)
{
  double p; // temporary variable
  p = price - cost; // calculate the profit
  return p; // return the result to the calling function
}
```

Great, now that you have a grasp of the three major parts of basic functions we can move on to other related material!

The functions we just described are known as **programmer defined functions** since the programmer defines these functions. There are also **predefined functions** which are available for your convenience. Predefined functions are functions that are already written and defined. In order to use predefined functions, the programmer needs to include the necessary library and then call the function wherever they need it.

In the following example we will use the `sqrt()` function to calculate the square root of the user's input. The `sqrt()` function is described in more detail in Chapter 17.

```
#include <iostream>
#include <cmath>
using namespace std;
int main()
{
  double num;
  cout << "Please enter a number: ";
  cin >> num;
  cout << sqrt(num) << endl;
  return 0;
}
```

14.3 `void` Functions

`void` functions are functions that do not return a value. Notice that other function declarations that do return a value start with their return type such as `double`, `int`, or the like. `void` functions behave the same except no value is returned. A common application where a `void` function is used is printing the result of calculations to the screen. The calculations might be performed elsewhere, but the results would be printed using the `void` function. Syntax for `void` functions works in the same way as normal functions, but the keyword `void` is written where the return data type would normally go. The declaration, function call and definition for `void` functions will follow the same format as other functions. Note that, like other functions, there does not necessarily need to be parameters in a `void` function. Here is an example of a simple `void` function declaration:

```
void displayMessage();
```

Remember the definition and calling of `displayMessage()` would be the same as any other function with the exception of the `void` return type and that no value is returned! Here is an example of a definition, declaration, and how this function would be called:

```cpp
#include <iostream>
using namespace std;

void displayMessage();

int main()
{
  int x = 2, y;
  y = x + 1;

  // This doesn't return anything
  displayMessage();

  return 0;
}

void displayMessage()
{
  cout << "Calculations are done!" << endl;
}
```

14.4   Overloading Function Names

Overloading function names allows the same name to be used in multiple function definitions but with different parameter listings. Function names can be reused using this feature. Function name overloading eliminates problems associated with having multiple names for functions with similar purposes and can make the code both more understandable and more convenient for the programmer to write.

Below is an example of an overloaded function name. Notice that both functions have the same name, but different parameter types.

```
int plus(int num, int numr);
float plus(float num, float numr);
```

Here is an example of improper function overloading. Simply changing the return type does not work—the parameters must be different!

```
int plus(int num, int numr);
float plus(int num, int numr);
```

14.5 Scope

As we dive into more complex programs there is a need for a wide variety of variables in different locations in the code. Some of these variables are declared within individual blocks of code, such as within loops or conditionals. Others are declared completely outside functions. The two primary types of variables we are going to look at here are local and global. The location of the declaration of a variable within the code changes how that variable may be used.

Local variables are declared within a block of code. A local variable is available to code from the point of its declaration through the end of that block of code. A simple example is a variable declared in main():

```
int main()
{
    int games;
    return 0;
}
```

The variable games is a **local variable** because it exists only within the local function, main(). It cannot be used anywhere outside main() without some additional work (such as passing it by reference to a function). Similarly, variables declared in other functions are not available to code in main().

```
#include <iostream>
using namespace std;

void my_games();

int main()
{
  my_games();
  cout << games; // ERROR! No such variable here!
  return 0;
}

void my_games()
{
  int games = 10;
  cout << games;
}
```

In the previous example function, my_games() is called by main() and outputs 10. The variable games is local to that function. If games is referenced anywhere else outside that function, the program will not compile.

An easy way to understand local variables is to compare them to your neighbors. Everyone that lives on your street and around you are variables, and since you all share the same street, they are local. The neighbors on an adjacent street might be close to where you live, but since they do not share the same street, they might not be considered neighbors. You can think of these neighbors on the adjacent street as other functions. While they might be close by, they do not share the same street.

Global variables are quite different from local variables. Global variables can be used by code anywhere within the program. A global variable is declared outside of any function. Using similar code as in the example above, we make the games variable global:

```
#include <iostream>
using namespace std;

int games;
void my_games();
void their_games();

int main()
{
  games = 5;
  my_games();
  their_games();
  return 0;
}

void my_games()
{
  cout << games << endl;
}

void their_games()
{
  cout << games << endl;
}
```

Both functions print the same variable, causing the program to produce the following output:

5
5

To sum it up, local variables work only within the block of code that it is declared. Global variables are declared outside functions, and can be used at any point in the program.

14.6 Review Questions

1. What are the three parts of a function?

2. Can a void function return a value?

3. How many functions can one program have?

4. What is the output of the following code snippet?

```cpp
#include <iostream>
using namespace std;

void example();

int main()
{
    return 0;
}
void example()
{
    cout << "Hello World";
}
```

5. Write code using at least one function that will ask the user to guess a "magic" number (of your choice) between 1 and 100 until they get it right. After a guess, the program should output whether the number they guessed is higher or lower than the "magic" number. It should also display how many guesses the user makes, and loop until the guess is correct.

6. Using at least one function, write code that prompts the user for a number of miles travelled and a number of hours, then calculates the user's speed in miles per hour.

14.7   Review Answers

1. Return type, function name, parameter(s)

2. No

3. As many as you want

4. There is no output

5.

```cpp
#include <iostream>
using namespace std;
void guessing_game();

int main() {
  guessing_game();
}

void guessing_game() {
  int guess, counter = 0, number = 5;
  bool found = false;
  do {
    cout << "Guess a number:\t";
    cin >> guess;
    if (guess > 100 or guess <= 0)
    {
      cout << "Number is between 1 and 100!\n\n";
      counter++;
    }
    else if (guess < number)
    {
      cout << "Too low. Guess again.\n\n";
      counter++;
    }
    else if (guess > number)
    {
      cout << "Too high. Guess again.\n\n";
      counter++;
    }
    else // guess == number
    {
      cout << "You got it!\n";
      found = true;
      counter++;
    }
  } while (!found);
  cout << "It took you " << counter << " guesses!\n";
  cout << "Thanks for playing!\n\n";
}
```

6.

```cpp
#include <iostream>
using namespace std;
double mph(double miles, double hours);

int main()
{
  double miles = 0, hours = 0, milesPerHour;
  cout << "Enter the number of miles traveled: ";
  cin >> miles;
  cout << "Enter the travel time in hours: ";
  cin >> hours;
  cout << "Your speed in miles per hour: "
    << mph(miles, hours);
  return 0;
}

double mph(double miles, double hours)
{
  return miles/hours;
}
```

14.8   Further Reading

- http://www.cplusplus.com/doc/tutorial/functions/
- http://www.cplusplus.com/doc/tutorial/functions2/
- http://www.cprogramming.com/tutorial/lesson4.html

Chapter 15

Problem Solving & Troubleshooting

Problem solving and troubleshooting in programming is often referred to as debugging. Does your program not compile? Does it not achieve the desired effect? Debugging is your answer. And, unless you are a perfect programmer, you are likely to do quite a bit of debugging. The first step to debugging is looking for common errors.

15.1   The Compilation Error

These errors happen when your compiler returns an error message after you hit compile. The messages usually tell you what is wrong, and what line the error is on, but be sure to double-check the lines immediately before and after the reported error. Because the code is incorrect, the compiler can only guess at what you meant and give you a hint.

For example, one of the most common errors a beginning programmer will encounter is forgetting a semicolon. In some development environments (like NetBeans in Figure 15.1), this will cause the error to be reported not on the line with the missing semicolon, but on the following line.

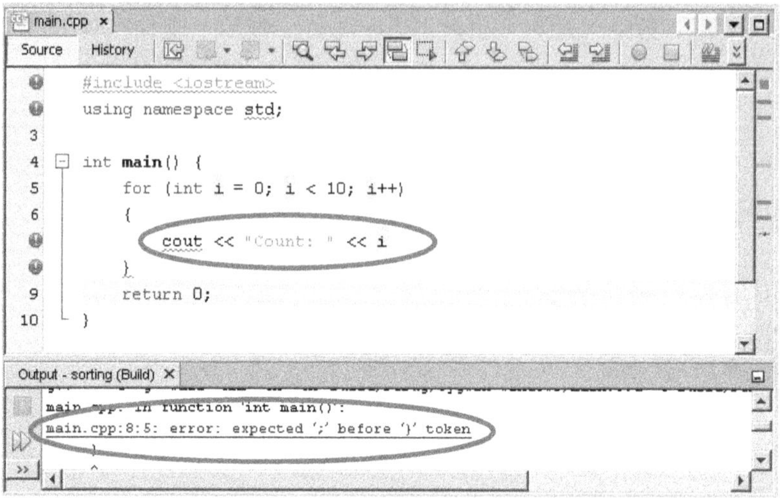

Figure 15.1: A syntax error in the NetBeans development environment

15.2   The Logic Error

Logic errors are often subtle, and occur after the code compiles. When the code is executed, however, the result is wrong. This may happen when arithmetic operators like +, -, *, and / get mixed up. Another common issue is misplacement of parentheses, as a misplaced parenthesis can cause problems in complex expressions.

15.3   The Infinite Loop

Another specific logic error is the infinite loop. The infinite loop is a common error that can result in your program repeating the same block of code over and over.

For an infinite loop to occur, the conditional expression of a `while`, `for`, or `do-while` loop remains true. There are many ways for this to happen, such as accidentally using = instead of == to compare two numbers, or using the wrong operators, like a > in the place of a <.

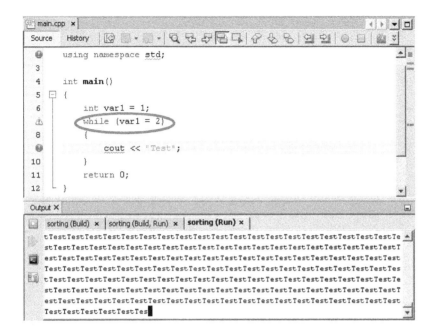

Figure 15.2: An infinite loop in the NetBeans development environment

15.4 Review Questions

1. Consider the following function:

   ```
   double average (double s1, double s2, double s3, s4);
   {
     retun s1+s2+s3+s4/4
   }
   ```

   (a) Find the syntax errors in the function.

   (b) There is a logic error in the function. What is it? How does it affect the output of the code?

2. The below program compiles, but does not get the result the programmer

wanted. Why?

```
int main ()
{
    int shots , goals , saves ;
    double save_perc ;
    char cont ;

    cout . unsetf ( ios :: fixed ) ;
    cout . unsetf ( ios :: showpoint ) ;
    cout << "Enter the number of shots on goal :\ t";
    cin >> shots ;
    cout << "Enter the number of goals scored :\ t";
    cin >> goals ;
    cout << endl ;

    saves = shots - goals ;
    // Hockey shows save % as decimal to three places
    save_perc = ( saves / shots ) ;
    cout << "If there were " << shots << " shots and "
        << goals << " goals , "
        << "then the goalie 's save percentage was ";

    cout . setf ( ios :: fixed ) ;
    cout . setf ( ios :: showpoint ) ;
    cout . precision (3) ;

    cout << save_perc << endl << endl ;
    return 0;
}
```

15.5   Review Answers

1.   (a) retun should be return. There is an extra semicolon at the end
        of the function header, and one missing after the return statement.

     (b) There are no parentheses around the addition, so s4 will be divided
        by 4, then added to s1 + s2 + s3, instead of adding all four
        variables and then dividing the sum by 4.

2.   Remove the unused variable cont and cout.unsetf lines. Because
     shots and goals are both integers, the program does the math as though
     you are looking for an int result and doesn't store the fractional parts,
     even though it stores the result in a double. Change shots, goals,
     and saves to be of type double and the program will work as intended.

Chapter 16

The Preprocessor

Preprocessor directives are lines of code that are executed before the compilation of the code begins. These directives are like getting everyone in a room before starting a project or doing warmups before running a race. One of the most frequently-used preprocessor directives is #include.

When we want to include in our code a system library or some other file, we use the keyword #include followed by the library name or the file name. The way we distinguish between including libraries and including files is with angle brackets and quotes, respectively. For example, when we want to use objects like cout or cin, we need to include the iostream library like so:

```
#include <iostream>
```

If we want to include a file, such as a file named myFile.h, we can write:

```
#include "myFile.h"
```

However, when we include files, they must be in the same directory as the file where the #include appears. We discuss the Standard Template Library in Chapter 23, and include a short sample of other libraries in Table 16.1.

Library	Provides	Some common uses
`<iostream>`	Input/output stream objects	`cout`, `cin`: see Chapters 6 and 5
`<cstdlib>`	The C standard library	`rand()`, `abs()`, `NULL`
`<cmath>`	Mathematical functions	`pow()`, `sqrt()`, `cos()`, `tan()`, `sin()`: see Chapter 17
`<iomanip>`	Input/output manipulation	`set_iosflags()`, `setfill()`, `setprecision()`
`<ctime>`	Time-related functions	`clock()`, `time()`
`<string>`	The string class	See Chapter 11
`<fstream>`	File input and output streams	See Chapter 18

Table 16.1: Some useful libraries and a sampling of what they provide

16.1   Review Questions

1. Which of the following demonstrate correct syntax for `#include` statements? (Note: some of these may be syntactically correct but not do what you would expect!)

   (a) `#include <aFile.txt>`

   (b) `#include <iostream>;`

   (c) `include <iostream>`

   (d) `#include myFile.txt;`

   (e) `#include "myFile.txt"`

   (f) `#include <cmath>;`

   (g) `include <cmath>`

   (h) `include "cmath"`

(i) `#include <cmath>`

(j) `#include (iostream);`

(k) `#include <iostream>`

2. Identify the the preprocessor statements in the following code:

```
#include <cstdlib >
#include <iostream >
using namespace std;
int main(int argc, char *argv[])
{
  cout << "Included!" << endl;
  return 0;
}
```

3. Which library is required to use the cout object?

4. Is using namespace std; a preprocessor directive?

5. If you want to be able to use the funtion pow(), which library do you need?

16.2 Review Answers

1. **a**, **e**, **i**, and **k**.

2. The first two lines are preprocessor directives.

3. The iostream library.

4. No.

5. The cmath library.

Chapter 17

Advanced Arithmetic

Advanced arithmetic in C++ includes mathematics that can't be used in code without the use of the <cmath> library. This is mathematics that goes above and beyond the primitive operations: addition (+), subtraction (-), multiplication (*), and division (/). As we have seen before, some simple arithmetic might look like:

```
int x;
x = 1;
x += 5;
```

The variable x is declared as an integer. The next line sets it to one. The += operator adds five to x, which makes x contain six. Doing simple operations like these does not require any special libraries or unusual commands. Any compiler can look at a +, -, *, or / in a line of code and know exactly what the programmer expects to happen. Some math requires a little extra help, though. In this case, help is the <cmath> library.

<cmath> is a library that is needed for trigonometric, hyperbolic, exponential, logarithmic, rounding, and absolute value functions. The <cmath> library is designed to make your life simple and to make complicated mathematics easier in C++. Using the <cmath> library in code is as simple as including it at the top of your source code file with the rest of your libraries. For example:

```
#include <iostream>
#include <cmath>
```

After the inclusion of the <cmath> library, you can use certain mathematical functions in your code such as pow(x, y), which raises the parameter x to the

97

power of parameter y, and `sqrt(z)`, which returns the square root of z. In your first few C++ programs you will probably not use the more advanced mathematical functions included in the `<cmath>` library, but for a full list of the functions provided in `<cmath>`, refer to "Further Reading" at the end of this chapter.

17.1 Examples

17.1.1 pow()

pow is the function called when you want to raise a value or variable to a certain power. Take a look at the code below and we'll break it down line by line.

```
int x, y;
x = 4;
y = pow(x + 1, 3) + 6;
```

First, we are declaring two variables: x and y. After that we set x to 4. Now we get to a more interesting section of code. We are asking the compiler to raise the value of x plus 1 to the power of 3, add 6, and then place the result in y. To use the pow function, you must understand its syntax. Here is the breakdown:

```
pow (starting value, power being raised)
```

In `pow(x + 1, 3) + 6`, we are raising the starting value x + 1 to the power of 3. Before the power of 3 is applied, 1 is added to x. In this case it is the simple operation of 4+1, which yields 5. After we get 5, we raise it to the 3rd power to get a value of 125. After we reach the value of 125 we are finished with the pow function and resume using normal operators when we add 6 to 125 resulting in the final value of 131.

Undoubtedly there are more complicated uses of the pow function, such as multiple uses of pow in the same line of code. You might use multiple pow operations in code that calculates the length of one side of a triangle using the Pythagorean Theorem. Look at the following code and see if you can figure out what the output value would be:

```
int x, y, z;
x = 3;
y = x + 1;
z = pow(x, 2) + pow(y, 2);
cout << z;
```

If you got 25, then you have the right answer! After initializing the variables x and y and setting their values (3 for x and x+1 for y), we raise each value to the power of 2. For visual reference,

```
z = pow (3, 2) + pow (x+1, 2);
```

results in

```
z = 9 + 16;
```

z's value is set to 25. The pow function is simple to use and can make the program simpler from a readability standpoint.

17.1.2 sqrt()

Square roots are calculated using the sqrt function. Take a look at the example below to see how it is called in a program:

```
int a, b;
a = 25;
b = sqrt(a);
```

sqrt is simpler than pow in that it only requires one parameter. Since sqrt returns a double, you should usually assign the result to a double variable, but in this example, sqrt returns exactly 5, so it is implicitly converted to an int without any issues.

There are cases where both sqrt and pow are used in the same formula, such as when calculating the distance between two points. When writing such code, it is very important to keep track of the parentheses and to use correct syntax. One such syntax mistake is made when programmers think that C++ syntax is the same as algebraic syntax. This is *not* the case in C++!

```
int x = (5)(pow(3, 3)); // Incorrect syntax!
```

When the compiler sees this, it doesn't view it as multiplication, but instead as (according to a professional), "function shenanigans." It is important to be explicit with mathematical symbols in C++. So instead of the incorrect code above, use:

```
int x = 5 * (pow (3, 3));
```

As an example, we will use code to compute the distance between the two points $(4, 4)$ and $(6, 10)$ on a plane.

```
int x1, x2, y1, y2;
float dist;
x1 = 4;
y1 = 4;
x2 = 6;
y2 = 10;

dist = sqrt(pow (x2 - x1, 2) + pow (y2 - y1, 2));
cout << dist;
```

Your final answer after the calculation is executed is roughly 6.342555. Without the help of the advanced arithmetic operations, getting to this result would be a difficult, long, drawn-out process. pow and sqrt are handy functions that make life easier, all with the help of the <cmath> library.

17.1.3 Modulo

The modulo operator (the percent sign: %) finds the remainder, or what was left over from division. This program uses the modulo operator to find all prime numbers (all the numbers that never have a remainder of 0 when divided by every number except 1 and itself) that can be held by an int.

```
#include <iostream>
using namespace std;
int main()
{
  int divby, remainder;
  for (int test = 1; test < 2147483647; test++)
  {
    bool isprime = true;
    for(divby = 2; divby < test; divby++)
    { // Store the remainder of testprime/divby
      remainder = test % divby;
      if (remainder == 0) // If the number is not prime
      {
        isprime = false;
        break; // Leave the for loop
      }
    }
    if (isprime) // If it passes the test, it is prime.
      cout << " " << testprime; // Print the prime
  }
  return 0;
}
```

17.2 Review Questions

1. Which #include library is needed to use advance arithmetic operators?

2. Write C++ code to calculate 2^9.

3. Write a statement to set the value of a variable of type double to the square root of 10001.

4. Complete the code below to find the length of the hypotenuse of a right triangle (remember that $a^2 + b^2 = c^2$) given the lengths of the other two sides. What is the final output of your code?

```
#include <iostream>
// Add necessary libraries here

using namespace std;

int main()
{
  double a = 3.0, b = 4.0;
  double c;
  //
  // Finish the program...
  //
  cout << "The hypotenuse of the right triangle is "
       << c << endl;
}
```

17.3 Review Answers

1. #include <cmath> must be included to include advanced operators.

2. pow(2, 9)

3. double b = sqrt(10001);

4.
```cpp
#include <iostream>
#include <cmath>

using namespace std;

int main()
{
  float a = 3.0, b = 4.0;
  double c;

  a = pow(a, 2);
  b = pow(b, 2);
  c = sqrt(a+b);

  cout << "The hypotenuse of the right triangle is "
       << c << endl;
}
```

The final output of the code is:

The hypotenuse of the right triangle is 5.0

17.4   Further Reading

- http://pages.cpsc.ucalgary.ca/~jacob/Courses/Fall00/CPSC231/Slides/08-Arithmetic.pdf
- http://www.cplusplus.com/reference/cmath/

Chapter 18

File I/O

File I/O refers to the input and output (I/O) from and to files. So far we have been using cin to get input from the keyboard and cout to output to the screen. Just like output can be sent to the screen, output can be sent to a file. Input can be taken either from a keyboard or from a file. Input and output is handled in the program through objects called **streams**. This chapter will discuss how to take input from a file and send output to the same file or a different one.

File I/O is useful because files provide a way to store data permanently. With keyboard input and screen output, the data is temporary and goes away once the program is finished. When it comes to files, the data is there for us and we do not have to waste our time typing it over and over again.

18.1   I/O Streams

If data is flowing into your program it is called an **input stream**. If data is flowing out of the program it is called an **output stream**. We have actually been using both types of streams already! cin, which handles a flow of data from the keyboard, is an input stream and cout, which produces a flow of data to the screen, is an output stream. If an input stream object is connected to a file, then the program can get its input from that file. Similarly, an output stream object can send data to the screen or to a file. A file can be opened for both reading and writing, in which case it can be accessed by both input and output streams.

18.2   File I/O

When the program opens a file for input, the program is reading from the file. When the program opens a file for output, the program is writing to the file. C++ provides us with the `ifstream`, `ofstream`, and `fstream` classes for reading from and writing to files. All of these classes are available through the `fstream` library, which means we must `#include` it in our code in order to use them:

```
#include <fstream>
```

The `ofstream` type (read that as "output file **stream**") is used to write data to files. The `ifstream` type ("input file **stream**") is used to read data from files. Objects of type `fstream` ("file **stream**") can combine the behavior of `ifstream` and `ofstream` and allow us to both read from and write to files.

The `cin` and `cout` objects are already declared for you. However, in order to use `ifstream`, `ofstream` and `fstream` objects, you must declare one like you would any other variable. Declaring these objects looks like this:

```
// Declares a variable of type ifstream named input
ifstream inFile;
// Declares a variable of type ofstream named output
ofstream outFile;
```

The variable `inFile` will deal with getting input from a file, while the variable `outFile` will deal with outputting data to a file.

Every file on a computer has its own name and a location (or **path**). An example of a text file name is `TextFile.txt` and its location in a Windows operating system might be `c:\storage\TextFile.txt`. In a UNIX-based operating system, the same file might be in `/home/user1/TextFile.txt`. Regardless of the operating system, we need to know the file's path in order to tell the program where to find the file.

18.3   Opening and closing a File

Before we can even start reading from and writing to a file we must open it. In order to open a file you must first make an object of type `ifstream`, `ofstream`, or `fstream` just like we did earlier. We open a file using a member function named `open`. The `ofstream` object will create a file for you if the file you're opening for output does not exist. Otherwise, if the file already exists, the `open` function will erase existing data in the file by default. The following example demonstrates how to open files for both input and output:

```
#include <iostream> //For cin and cout
#include <fstream> // For ifstream and ofstream
using namespace std;
int main ()
{
    //Declares a variable of type ifstream called inFile
    ifstream inFile;
    //Declares a variable of type ofstream called outFile
    ofstream outFile;

    //Opens text file for input
    inFile.open("TextFile.txt");
    //Creates text file for output
    outFile.open("OutputTextFile.txt");

    return 0;
}
```

Once you are done with the file, it is good practice to close it. Closing the file disconnects it from the program and prevents the program from continuing to read from or write to the file. If the program ends normally or crashes, the files will be automatically closed. Closing files is even simpler than opening them. All you need to do is use the close function with empty parentheses. For example, to close both inFile and outFile:

```
inFile.close();
outFile.close();
```

18.4 Reading from a File

We use the ifstream class to read data from a file. Instead of having a user input data from the keyboard, we now input the data from a file. As you recall from earlier in the book, we used cin with >>, the **extraction operator**. This is the operator we use when we would like get input from the keyboard and it is also used with ifstream objects. Once we have declared our variable of type ifstream and opened a file, we can use it to input data. Using this is very similar to cin except we replace c in with the name of our variable. For example:

```
#include <iostream>
#include <fstream>
using namespace std;
int main()
{
    int number = 5;
    ifstream inFile;

    inFile.open("TextFile.txt");

    inFile >> number;
    // The value 5 in number is overwritten
    // by the integer stored in the file

    return 0;
}
```

This will read in one integer from the file and store it into the variable num-ber. You can input all different types of data including characters, doubles, and floats. Overall, ifstream objects are very similar to cin—you just have to declare one and remember to use the variable name instead of cin.

18.5   Writing data to a File

We use the ofstream class to output data to files. cout outputs data to our screen whereas ofstream stores data in files. Just like cout, ofstream objects use <<, the **insertion operator**. Using this is very similar to cout except we replace the cout with the name of our variable. For example:

```cpp
#include <iostream>
#include <fstream>
using namespace std;
int main ()
{
   char Letter = 'A';
   ofstream outFile;

   outFile.open("OutputTextFile.txt");

   outFile << Letter; // Puts the letter 'A' into the file

   return 0;
}
```

This example would write the letter 'A' to the text file we created named OutputTextFile.txt. You can also create numeric variables and output them to the file just like:

```cpp
int num = 10;
outFile << num << endl;
```

This example would output the number 10 and create a new line in the text file we created.

18.6 Introduction to Classes and Objects

We will go into more detail about classes and objects in Chapter 21 but it is necessary to go over it briefly in this section. Both cin and cout are objects. An **object** is a variable that has functions built in and may have multiple pieces of data associated with it. ifstream and ofstream are object types that define which operations may be performed on and which data are stored in the objects. For example, the function open() (along with close() and many others) is considered a **member function** of ifstream and ofstream, which means it is a function that is associated with object of those two types. Getting a little more into detail, these object types are defined as part of a **class**. A class is a blueprint for complex data types. We already know data types such as integers, doubles, and chars, but using classes, you will be able to design your own data type.

When calling the functions open or close, you will notice we use a period between the object name and the function. We call this the **dot operator** and it is used to reference member functions and member variables of a class.

18.7   Other functions

The <fstream> library comes with many functions to help test to see if things are working. One example is the fail() function. We use this function to determine whether the file was opened successfully or not. We usually use if statements with the function so that if the file does not open correctly we can warn the user. For example:

```
inFile.open("TextFile.txt");
if (inFile.fail())
{
    cout << "Failed to open!";
}
```

This will warn the user if the file did not open correctly. If the file *did* open correctly, the program would continue without printing the error message.

The next function is the eof() (**end** of **f**ile) function. This function tests to see if the stream has reached the end of the file. This function is very useful in order to know when to stop reading from the file. For example:

```
int number;
inFile.open("TextFile.txt");
while (!inFile.eof())
{
    inFile >> number
}
```

This example shows how the eof() function can be used in a while loop. The while loop will read integers from the file until the program reaches the end of the file. This is useful for gathering all the data from one file.

The get() and put() functions are used to read and write single characters, respectively. The function get() allows the program to read in a single character into a variable of type char. When we use the >> operator, spaces, tabs and new-lines—the whitespace characters—around data are skipped automatically. However with get(), nothing is done automatically, so the whitespace characters can be extracted, too. The member function get() takes one argument in parentheses that must be a char variable. For example:

```
char Character;
ifstream inFile;

cin.get(Character);
// or
inFile.get(Character);
```

This will read in the next character typed on the keyboard or from the file. Even if the next character is a space, tab, or newline, the program will store that character in the variable.

The put() function is used to output one character. This function takes one argument of type char in the parentheses. For example:

```
char Character = '\n'; // newline character
ofstream outFile;

cout.put(Character);
// or
outFile.put(Character);
```

18.8 Review Questions

1. What do we call the type of object used to control data flowing into your program?

2. What do we call the type of object used to control data flowing out of your program?

3. What header file must you #include in order to use ifstream and ofstream?

4. What are ifstream and ofstream used for?

5. How do you declare an ifstream object named input and an ofstream object named output?

6. How would you open a file named TextFile.txt with an ifstream object called input?

7. How would you close a file named TextFile.txt with an ofstream object called output?

8. What kind of function is the eof() function and what does it do?

9. What are the benefits of using files for input and output?

10. What is the difference between cin >> c; and cin.get(c); if c is of type char?

11. Write a program that outputs the contents of some file to the screen.

12. Write a program that reads in a text file and prints to the screen the number of times the character 'e' shows up.

18.9   Review Answers

1. An input stream

2. An output stream

3. You need to `#include <fstream>`

4. `ifstream` is used to read data from a file. `ofstream` is used to write data to a file.

5. `ifstream input;`
   `ofstream output;`

6. `input.open("TextFile.txt");`

7. `output.close();`

8. The `eof()` function is a member function. It returns `true` if the program has reached the end of the file.

9. File input and output are useful because files provide a way to store data permanently. With keyboard input and screen output, the data is temporary and disappears once the program is finished. The data stored in files on the other hand remains the same until another program changes it. Also, an input file can be used by many programs at the same time without having to store multiple copies or re-enter the data over and over again.

10. The first `cin` statement the next non-whitespace character into `c`, but the call to `cin.get()` stores the next character in `c` whether it is whitespace or not.

18.10   Further Reading

- http://www.cprogramming.com/tutorial/lesson10.html
- http://www.cplusplus.com/doc/tutorial/files/
- http://www.tutorialspoint.com/cplusplus/cpp_files_streams.htm

Chapter 19

Pointers

Pointers do just what they sound like they do. They point to a space in memory, usually a location occupied by a variable. A pointer is an address in memory. The pointer itself is a variable, but it also refers to a variable. It is declared using an asterisk following the data type:

```
int *ptr;
```

The variable named `ptr` is of type `int*`, an "integer pointer" that stores the address of a variable of type `int`.

To indicate that a pointer variable is not pointing toward any usable data, we often set its value to NULL, which is defined as zero when you `#include <cstdlib>`:

```
int *ptr = NULL;
```

C++11 provides a dedicated null pointer object called `nullptr` that can be used similarly:

```
int *ptr = nullptr;
```

There are two operators used in conjunction with pointers. The `*` operator, beyond being used for multiplication and for pointer declarations, also acts as the **dereference operator**. The dereference operator changes the pointer into the value it is pointing to. It "follows" the address stored in the pointer and returns whatever is in that location.

The & operator is the **reference operator**. The dereference operator returns the memory address of the variable it precedes. You will use this to produce a pointer

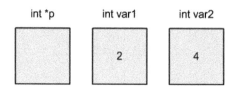

Figure 19.1: The state of the variables after lines 1-3

to the indicated variable. Let's declare pointer p and use it:

```
int *p;        // Declare an int pointer
int var1 = 2;  // Declare an int, set it to 2
p = &var1;     // Take the address of var1 and store it in p
cout << *p;    // Go to the address stored in p;
               // return the value; print it out
```

The output of this code is:
2

Here is a slightly longer example:

```
int *p;
int var1 = 2;
int var2 = 4;
p = &var1; // Take the address of var1 and store it in p
*p = var2; // Go to the address stored in p;
           // assign it the value stored in var2

// The preceding two lines are equivalent to var1 = var2
cout << *p << endl;
cout << var1 << endl;
cout << var2 << endl;
```

The output of this code is:
4
4
4

Figure 19.1 shows the state of the variables in the second example after they are declared and initialized (lines 1-3). After the fourth line is executed, p will store the address of var1. Figure 19.2 shows the state of the variables. After the fifth line of code is executed, the location where p points is assigned the value stored in var2. Since p contains the address of var1, var1 receives that value. Figure

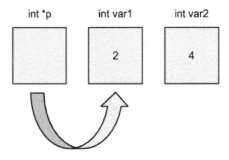

Figure 19.2: The state of the variables after line 4

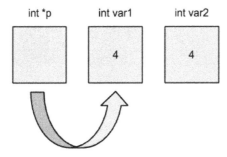

Figure 19.3: The state of the variables after line 5

19.3 shows the state of the variables.

Use caution when declaring pointers. If you are declaring more than one pointer in a single line, make sure to indicate each pointer variable with the * before the variable name. Here is a correct declaration of two pointers:

```
int *p, *q;
```

This results in an integer pointer named p and an integer pointer named q. Contrast that with the below code:

```
int *p, q;
```

This results in an integer pointer named p and an integer named q. An equivalent way to write the above is:

```
int q, *p;
```

19.1 Review Questions

1. What is the output of the following code?

```
int *a, b, c;
a = &b;
b = 5;
c = 1;
b = b - b;
c = b * b;
*a = c - *a;
a = &c;
*a = c - 7;
c = c + c;
*a = *a + b;
c = c + b;
b = c - 3;
c = *a - 7;
cout << *a << endl;
cout << b << endl;
cout << c << endl;
```

2. What is the output of the following code?

```
int a, b, *c;
a = 7;
b = 4;
c = &a;
a = *c - a;
*c = *c + 4;
a = b + a;
c = &b;
a = a - b;
*c = b + a;
*c = *c - 1;
a = a * 1;
a = b - *c;
a = a - *c;
cout << a << endl;
cout << b << endl;
cout << *c << endl;
```

19.2 Review Answers

1. -21
   -17
   -21

2. -7
   7
   7

Chapter 20

Dynamic Data

Up to this point, we have only discussed variables that are set up at compile time. Allocating space for variables at compile time is adequate in many cases, but occasionally a program will need to allocate space for data in memory while it is running. Consider the following code:

```
int arraySize;
cout << "Enter the number of elements in your array: ";
cin >> arraySize;
// We want to create an array with arraySize elements
int myArray[arraySize]; // SYNTAX ERROR!
```

In order to allocate the space for `myArray`, the compiler needs to know how many elements make up the array so that there is enough room in memory to accommodate the array. Unfortunately, the value of `arraySize` is not known until the user enters something on the keyboard *after the program has started running* and as a result, the compiler returns a syntax error.

In C++, pointers are used to keep track of dynamically-allocated data:

```
float *fPtr = NULL; // (1) Declare a pointer to a float,
                    // which currently points nowhere
```

In order to dynamically allocate an object of type `float`, we use the `new` operator:

```
fPtr = new float; // (2)
```

The created object of type `float` does not have a name, so the `new` operator

117

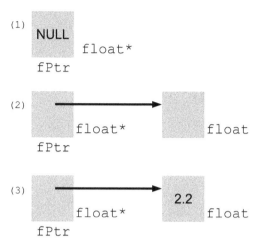

Figure 20.1: Allocation and dereferencing of pointers

returns a float* that can be used to access the object. This pointer is stored in fPtr. We use the dereference operator (*, that is) to access the data:

```
*fPtr = 2.2;  // (3) Goes to address at fPtr & puts 2.2 there
cout << "Data at " << fPtr << ": " << *fPtr << endl;
// This outputs: Data at 0x200102b0:  2.2
// Note that the address listed may differ
// Also note the difference between printing fPtr and *fPtr
```

Notice that when a value is assigned to fPtr, the pointer is being changed. When a value is assigned to *fPtr (notice the dereference operator), the floating-point value at the address stored in fPtr is changed.

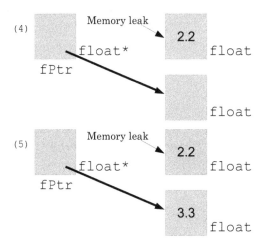

Figure 20.2: Allocation and memory leaks

```
float *fPtr;
fPtr = new float;
*fPtr = 2.2; // Goes to address at fPtr & puts 2.2 there
cout << "Data at " << fPtr << ": " << *fPtr << endl;
fPtr = new float; // (4) fPtr now holds address of
                  //     a new float object
*fPtr = 3.3; // (5)
cout << "Data now at " << fPtr << ": " << *fPtr << endl;
// This outputs:
// Data at 0x200102b0: 2.2
// Data now at 0x200483c0: 3.3
```

In this example, the float containing the value 2.2 still resides in memory, but is no longer reachable. This condition is called a **memory leak**, and results in programs that consume more memory than they require. In order to free up the memory properly, we use the `delete` operator:

```
float *fPtr;
fPtr = new float;
*fPtr = 2.2; // (6) Goes to the address at fPtr and stores
    2.2 there
cout << "Data at " << fPtr << ": " << *fPtr << endl;
delete fPtr; // (7) Frees up the dynamically-allocated
            // memory at the address stored in fPtr
```

At this point in the code, `fPtr` can be referred to as a **dangling pointer**, since the memory location it refers to is no longer valid, and the pointer just "dangles" there, pointing to nothing useful.

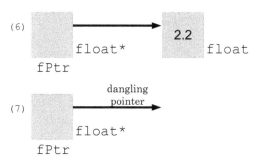

Figure 20.3: Deallocation and dangling pointers

Arrays can be dynamically allocated, too:

```
float *fPtr = new float[10]; // Allocate an array of ten
                // floats and store their location in fPtr
```

Arrays must be deleted in a similar fashion, but the syntax changes slightly:

```
delete [] fPtr; // Free up the entire array
```

20.1 Review Questions

1. Write code to declare an integer pointer and dynamically allocate an integer. On the next line, assign this dynamically-allocated integer the value 13.

2. Given the following code, write a few lines that deallocate any dynamically-allocated memory and set all pointer values to NULL:

```
int *a = new int [24];
int *b;
int c;
b = &c;
```

20.2 Review Answers

1.
```
int *iPtr = new int;
*iPtr = 13;
```

2.
```
delete [] a;
a = NULL;
b = NULL;
```

20.3 Further Reading

- http://www.cplusplus.com/doc/tutorial/dynamic/

Chapter 21

Classes and Abstraction

Imagine for a second you're behind the wheel of an automobile. You're driving along, but do you know your engine is working right if it's not making any horrendous screeching sounds? Do you have any idea how your steering actually works when you turn the wheel? So long as you can press down on the accelerator to move forward and the steering handles correctly, you probably don't care about the specifics of how things work.

Abstract data types (ADTs) are the automobiles of C++, and one of the reasons C++ is known as an **object-oriented programming language**. It's their job to package and obscure the information from the average user, and at the same time make their lives more convenient. ADTs can be thought of as a group of data of different types that are treated as a single item. For example, if we wanted to record the name, identification number, age, graduation date, and sex of all of the students on a campus, we could create a new data type named Student with those variables. In the following sections we will show you how to use and define two types of ADTs: structures and classes.

21.1 structs

A common example of a struct is a Point. Points store int, float, or double variables x and y, which represent the position of the Point on the the

123

X and Y axes on a coordinate plane. Such a struct might look like this:

```
struct Point
{
  double x;
  double y;
};
```

In the example, the keyword struct is used to declare the structure definition while the identifier, the word directly to the right of struct (Point), is the structure name and the name of a new data type. The braces are used just like when we define a function. However, directly after the closing brace, there must be a semicolon!

Once a structure is defined, it can be used just like the data types int, char, string, and so on. For example, we might declare a Point structure named input like this:

```
Point input;
```

21.2   Assigning values to member variables

Any variable of type Point such as the one above is a collection of two variables, x and y. Any variables contained in the struct can be accessed by combining the structure name—input in our example—followed by a symbol called the **dot operator** (the period, .) and the member variable's name. For example, if we wanted to set x in input, we would use the dot operator as follows:

```
input.x = 5;
```

21.3   Classes

classes are like structs except classes contain both variables and functions, whereas structs only contain variables.[1] Also, in a struct, member variables are public by default while all members of a class are private by default. We'll discuss the distinction more in a minute. First, let's take a look at an actual class definition.

---

[1]This has been the conventional way to think about classes and structs, but in reality the *only* difference between the two is that members of a struct are public by default and members of a class are private by default.

```
class Rectangle
{
public:
  Rectangle();   //A default constructor
  //The following two lines are mutators
  void setBase(float length);
  void setHeight(float length);
  //The following two lines are accessors
  float getHeight();
  float getBase();
  //The following two lines perform operations
  float findArea();
  float findPerimeter();
private:
  float Base;
  float Height;
};
```

Notice the similar syntax to the `struct`. Like a `struct`, the declaration starts with the `class` keyword, followed by the name of the `class`, and after the closing right brace, a semicolon. Notice the `public:` and `private:` sections of the definition. To indicate that a set of member variables or functions is private, we use the `private` keyword followed by a colon. Everything after the keyword will be considered private. We will discuss what this means in the next section.

On the other hand, if we want to indicate that a set a member variables or functions is public, we use the keyword `public` followed by a colon. Everything after this keyword will be considered public.

21.4 `public` and `private` variables and functions

The biggest difference between `class`es and `struct`s is the ability to determine how accessible the data within the class is. A general rule of thumb is to put variables in the `private:` section, where they would be referred to as private member variables, and related functions in the `public:` section, where they would be referred to as public member functions. Private members can only be accessed by the `class`'s member functions and nowhere else, while public members can be used anywhere, in the same way that the members of a `struct` can be used.

Within the above `class` definition, we have seven member functions that we need to define. Each function has a specific purpose to set the values of private member variables, return the values of private member variables, or perform some other operation using those member variables.

Functions that are declared in the above code with names starting with the word get will be used to access the variables; these functions are called **accessors**. Functions that are declared in the above code that have names starting with the word set will be used to change the variables' values; these functions are called **mutators**. Accessors and mutators can be named whatever you like, but it is a common convention to name them get and set plus the name of the variable you are accessing or mutating.

The functions whose names start with find perform operations using the variables, but do not change them or return their values directly. The function named Rectangle() is known as a **constructor**. When a Rectangle object is created, it will be initialized according to the code in this constructor. By the end of this chapter, you'll understand how useful these are in object-oriented programming.

21.5   Defining member functions

We now describe how to use member functions with private member variables. When we define a member function, all the member variables within the class are accessible to the function. For example, we can define the member function setBase() from Rectangle above like this:

```
void  Rectangle :: setBase ( float  length )
{
   Base = length ;
}
```

In this code, we are able to directly access the member variable Base because both the function setBase() and the member variable Base are a part of the class. Since we are not returning anything to the user, the function is defined as a void function. In order to define a member function, we have to use a special operator called the **scope resolution operator** (::). The function is defined by using the return type, the class name, scope resolution operator, then the member function name with any parameters listed just like any other non-class function.

21.6   Using member functions

All member functions have direct access to member variables even if the variable is private. The reason we use mutators is because we do not want the user to have direct access to any variables within the class—we give them indirect access instead. We do this by requiring them to pass a value to the mutator member function which sets the member variable. That might look like this:

```
int main()
{
  Rectangle r;
  float b;
  cout << "Please input the length of the base: ";
  cin >> b;
  r.setBase(b);
  return 0;
}
```

In the above code, we start by creating a Rectangle variable named r. After the user is prompted for the length of the base, which is stored in the variable b, we call the setBase() member function with the dot operator and pass b as a parameter to the function.

We are able to pass the value of the variable entered by the user to the setBase() function which then sets the member variable Base to the passed value. This is how we "mutate" private member variables in a class using a public member function.

To retrieve the value of a member variable, we need to create accessor functions. These are defined like this:

```
float Rectangle::getBase()
{
  return Base;
}
```

When it comes to using accessors, it is very simple. Just match the data type that you want to access, in this case it was a float, and define the member function with that return type. Then, in order to access the variable, all we need to do is use the keyword return followed by the identifier. This enables us to access the private variable when we need to.

21.7 classes and structs together

We can also combine structs and classes if need be. For example, if we wanted to take in three points we could create a Triangle class with these points which are individually of type Point, a struct that contains x and y variables:

```
struct Point
{
  double x;
  double y;
};

class Triangle
{
public:
// accessors for points a, b, and c
// mutators for points a, b, and c
private:
  Point a;
  Point b;
  Point c;
};
```

Here we have the ability to combine a struct with a class in order to have all three points, a, b, and c that each contain their own variables x and y. Despite the fact that the variables in the struct are public, we cannot access those specific values outside the Triangle unless we use a member function. This is because they're still private members of the class Triangle, so their scope is limited to functions within the class. If we had a mutator function for Point a, it might look like this:

```
void Triangle :: setA (double userX, double userY)
{
  a.x = userX;
  a.y = userY;
}
```

The values of userX and userY are passed in by the calling function. Notice again that in order to access the x and y coordinates, we must use the dot operator with any of the Point objects a, b, or c.

21.8   Constructors

Another way to set the values of the variables in a class is through constructors. A **constructor** is a member function with the same name as the class and cannot be called directly. Constructors are what we use to initialize the variables of the class when it's first created. For example, if we wanted to set default values for a class named student defined as:

```
class student
{
public:
  student();  // constructor
  // accessors
  // mutators
private:
  string name;
  int age;
  int grad_year;
  string id;
};
```

we would have a default constructor with the name student() without any return type. To initialize the variables in the class through the constructor, we use syntax similar to a function definition:

```
student::student()
{
  name = "N/A";
  age = 0;
  grad_year = 0;
  id = "A00000000";
}
```

21.9 Overloading Member Functions

Note that, like other functions, you can overload any of the functions in a class. Going back to the Rectangle example used earlier, take a look at the following code.

```
class Rectangle
{
public:
  Rectangle();   //A default constructor
  //Overloaded constructor
  Rectangle(float userBase, float userHeight);
  void setBase(float length);  //These two lines are mutators
  void setHeight(float length);
  float getHeight();   //These two lines are accessors
  float getBase();
  float findArea();  //These two lines perform operations
  float findPerimeter();
private:
  float Base;
  float Height;
};
```

Notice the second constructor, Rectangle(float userBase, float userHeight). We define it very similarly to the default constructor:

```
Rectangle::Rectangle(float userBase, float userHeight)
{
  Base = userBase;
  Height = userHeight;
}
```

21.10   Review Questions

1. Given the following struct definition and global variable:

```
struct personInfo
{
  string name;
  int birth_year;
  int birth_month;
  int birth_day;
  int age;
};

personInfo pinfo;
```

which of the following are incorrect ways to use the dot operator?

(a) pinfo.age

(b) `personInfo.birth_year`

(c) `information.name`

(d) `pinfo.(string name)`

(e) `birth_year.pinfo`

2. Create a `class` called `Animal` that can store information about animals in a zoo and has the following private variables:

```
string name;     // the name of the animal
int pounds;      // number of pounds of food eaten
char animalType; // the type of animal:
                 // 'h' for herbivore
                 // 'c' for carnivore
```

You should have public member functions that get and set each variable, and a function called `print()` that prints all the information about the animal.

3. This program will require a `struct` and a `class`.

Write a program that can calculate the slope of a line.

You will have a `struct` called `Point` which contain the following variables:

```
double x, y;
```

You will then have a class called `Line`, and it will have the following private variables:

```
Point a, b;
```

Your class should have accessor and mutator functions, a function that calculates and returns the slope of a line between the two `Point`s as a `double`, and a function that outputs the data to the user called `print()`.

21.11   Review Answers

1. Only (a) is correct: (b) through (e) will result in syntax errors.

2.
```
class Animal
{
public :
  Animal () ;
  string getName () ;
  void setName ( string inputName ) ;
  int getPounds () ;
  void setPounds ( int inputPounds ) ;
  char getType () ;
  void setType ( char inputType ) ;
  void print () ;

private :
  string name ;       // the name of the animal
  int pounds ;        // number of pounds of food eaten
  char animalType ;   // the type of animal
};
```

21.12   Further Reading

- http://pages.cpsc.ucalgary.ca/~jacob/Courses/Fall00/CPSC231/Slides/08-Arithmetic.pdf

- http://www.tutorialspoint.com/cplusplus/cpp_classes_objects.htm

- http://www.cprogramming.com/tutorial/lesson7.html

Chapter 22

Separate Compilation

Separate compilation is the process of breaking a C++ program into separate files to improve organization. Parts of the program can be spread out over a number of different files that are later compiled individually, then **linked** using a linker to produce the final, working program. When changes are made, only those files with changes need to be recompiled, the result of which can then be relinked with the previously-compiled files. This process is nearly invisible in most development environments, which recompile and relink these files automatically. When the development environment takes care of these details, the user is left with the sole task of making changes where they are needed.

One of the most basic applications of separate compilation is used when writing abstract data types. Recall from Chapter 21 that there are declaration and definition sections in a class. The declaration contains class functions and variables, both public and private, while the definition section is where the function definitions and most actual code can be found. The process of separate compilation requires the two sections to be split into separate files, each of which is written and maintained separately and later used together to create a working program.

Declarations will be put into the **interface** file or the **header file** which typically has a .h suffix. In most code written by novice programmers, there will be only one class declaration in each header file. To use the class in your code elsewhere, you should use #include followed by the file name in double quotes. Below is an example of the contents of an interface file called student.h.

```
#include <string>
using namespace std;

class student
{
public:
  student();
  int getAge();
  void setAge(int update);
  int getID();
  void setID(int update);
  string getName();
  void setName(string update);
private:
  int age;
  int ID;
  string name;
};
```

To use the student class in some other source code file, that file should include the following line:

```
#include "student.h"
```

The quotes around student.h tell the compiler to find the header file in the same directory as the current file.

The **implementation** file will include all the function definitions for the student class. The implementation file can be called anything the programmer wants, but typically ends with a .cpp suffix. For example, the implementation file for student will probably be student.cpp.

To ensure that a new implementation file is compiled into your program, you do not need to #include anything. However, the development environment will automatically compile and link the implementation file if it has been added to your project. The only files that you should #include are header files.

To avoid linker errors, your files should have safeguards to ensure that classes and functions are not declared more than once within the same program. These safeguards are simple, and should be included in each header file. For example, we place the following two lines at the top of the file student.h:

```
#ifndef STUDENT_H  // STUDENT_H could be anything
#define STUDENT_H  // as long as it is unique to this file
```

The following line should go at the end of the same file:

```
#endif //STUDENT_H — a reminder about the #ifndef above
```

The above three lines do the following:

1. Test if STUDENT_H has been previously #defined, usually because this header file has been #included elsewhere.

2. If it has not been #defined, #define it now and proceed with compiling the code between the #ifndef and #endif.

3. Close the #ifndef block. If STUDENT_H was previously defined, skip to the line after this one.

Here is an example of what these lines look like alongside some actual code:

```
#ifndef  STUDENT_H
#define  STUDENT_H

class student
{
//class declaration because this is an interface file
};

#endif //STUDENT_H
```

This combination of preprocessor directives will ensure that the student class is only defined once.

22.1 Review Questions

1. What is a header file?

2. What file extension do we typically use for a C++ header file?

3. What file extension do we typically use for a C++ implementation file?

4. In which file would would you typically store an abstract data type's (ADT's) declaration?

5. How do you incorporate a header file named something.h into a file named main.cpp?

6. Do you incorporate an implementation file into your project the same way?

7. How do you prevent redeclaration of ADTs and functions in header files?

22.2   Review Answers

1. A header file stores the interface of an ADT

2. A header file ends in `.h`

3. An implementation file ends in `.cpp`

4. In the interface file

5. Add #include `"something.h"` alongside the other #include statements in `main.cpp`.

6. No, the implementation file will automatically be compiled and linked by your development environment as long as the implementation file is in your project.

7. You prevent redeclaration by adding lines similar to the following to the top of your header file:

```
#ifndef  SOMETHING_H
#define  SOMETHING_H
```

Then add the following to the end of the header file:

```
#endif  // SOMETHING_H
```

22.3   Further Reading

- http://elm.eeng.dcu.ie/~ee402/ee402notes/html/ch03s14.html
- http://web-ext.u-aizu.ac.jp/~fayolle/teaching/2012/C++/pdf/1-separate_compilation.pdf

Chapter 23

STL

The Standard Template Library (STL) provides a set of tools beyond those that are provided by the "base" C++ language. While a comprehensive discussion of the features of the STL is far beyond the scope of this text, there are several libraries that offer extremely important features with which you should become comfortable. Note: rather than assuming that

```
using namespace std;
```

is at the top of every code example, each data type, function, or variable derived from the STL will be shown with the prefix `std::`. This highlights which parts of the examples below come from the STL, and which are part of the language.

23.1 #include <utility>
#include <tuple> (C++11)

The `pair` class, found in `<utility>`, links two values which may be of different types. The `tuple` class, introduced in C++11, links any number of values which may be of different types. For example, to link a student's identification number (an integer) and their grade point average (a `float`), we can write:

```
std::pair<int,float> grades = { 112233, 3.81 };
```

We can assign different values to the `pair` later with the `make_pair` function:

```
grades = std :: make_pair (123450, 2.79);
```

The `first` and `second` members are used to extract the individual components of the `pair`:

```
std :: cout << "ID: " << grades.first << " (GPA "
  << grades.second << ")" << std :: endl ;
// This prints :
// ID : 123450 (GPA 2.79)
```

If we wanted a more complicated set of values linked together, such as a student's name, identification number, grade point average, and major, we could construct the following:

```
tuple <std :: string , int , float , std :: string > ethan =
  { "Ethan Allen", 802802, 3.15, "Engineering"};
```

Unfortunately, the `tuple` class does not have `first` or `second` members. The first and second elements can be retrieved in a slightly more complicated way than with `pair` objects:

```
std :: cout << std :: get <0 >(ethan) << "'s major is "
  << std :: get <3 >(ethan) << std :: endl ;
// This prints :
// Ethan Allen 's major is Engineering
```

In the code below, the `get` function returns a reference to the third element (the GPA) of the `tuple` `ethan`, and sets that value to 3.99:

```
std :: get <2 >(ethan) = 3.99;
```

These types may not be all that useful by themselves, but are often used in conjunction with container classes like `vector` and `map`, described below.

23.2   #include <iterator>

Iterators are objects that refer to elements within a container object (like `std :: vector`, `std :: map`, and `std :: array`) and allow for traversal through those elements. The list of features in iterators vary depending on the container class. While the specifics of the iterators vary, most iterators belong to one of the following categories, based on the operations that may be performed on them.

23.2.1 Forward iterators

- Can be incremented to move forward in the container to the next item
- Can be dereferenced like a pointer variable

```
std :: array < int > myArray = { 5, 10, 15, 20, 25 };
std :: array :: iterator myIterator, arrayEnd;
arrayEnd = myArray.end();

// Demonstrating forward iteration
for (myIterator = myArray.begin();
     myIterator != arrayEnd;
     ++myIterator)
  std :: cout << *myIterator << " ";

std :: cout << std :: endl << "The end!" << std :: endl;

// This prints:
// 5  10  15  20  25
// The end!
```

23.2.2 Bidirectional iterators

- Everything a forward iterator can do and:
- Can be decremented to move backward in the container to the previous item

```
std :: array < int > myArray = { 5, 10, 15, 20, 25 };
std :: array :: iterator myIterator, arrayBegin;
arrayBegin = myArray.begin();

// Demonstrating backward iteration
for (myIterator = myArray.end();
     myIterator != arrayBegin;
     ——myIterator)
  std :: cout << *myIterator << " ";

std :: cout << std :: endl << "The beginning!" << std :: endl;

// This prints:
// 25  20  15  10  5
// The beginning!
```

23.2.3 Random access iterators

- Everything a bidirectional iterator can do and:

- Can use arithmetic operators to move forward and backward a certain number of items at once

- Allows comparisons between iterators to determine relative positions in the container

- Can use array-style access to elements in the container

```cpp
// Create an array of 5 integers
std::array<int, 5> myArray = { 5, 10, 15, 20, 25 };
std::array<int, 5>::iterator myIterator, arrayEnd;
arrayEnd = myArray.end();
myIterator = myArray.begin();

// Demonstrating random access
std::cout << myIterator[1] << " "
  << myIterator[3] << std::endl;

// Demonstrating iterator comparisons
if (myIterator < arrayEnd)
  std::cout << "Not at the end of the array yet!"
    << std::endl;

// Demonstrating arithmetic operations on an iterator
for (myIterator = myArray.begin();
     myIterator != arrayEnd;
     myIterator += 2)
  std::cout << *myIterator << " ";

std::cout << std::endl << "The end!" << std::endl;

// This prints:
// 10 20
// Not at the end of the array yet!
// 5 15 25
// The end!
```

23.3   #include <vector>

Vectors are containers similar to arrays that are flexible in size and quite fast. While we can use iterators as above, we can also treat the `vector` much like an array.

```
// Start with 10 elements, all with the value 98.6
std :: vector<float> temperatures(10, 98.6);

// The last element has a fever of 103.1 degrees!
temperatures[9] = 103.1;

for (int i = 0; i < temperatures.size(); i++)
{
   std :: cout << "Patient " << i << "'s temperature is "
      << temperatures[i] << std :: endl;
}
```

The `vector` class also provides member functions `front()` and `back()` which return references to the first element and the last element in the vector, respectively. For example:

```
std :: cout << "The last patient's temperature is "
   << temperatures.back() << std :: endl;
std :: cout << "The first patient's temperature is "
   << temperatures.front() << std :: endl;
```

Don't confuse the `back()` and `front()` functions with the `end()` and `begin()` functions. The `back()` and `front()` functions return references to the elements, while `end()` and `begin()` return *iterators* pointing to those elements.

23.4   #include <map>

This library provides one of the STL's associative container object classes. An associative container differs from an array in that items in an array are referenced with a number which indicates the item's position in memory:

```
int myArray[10]; // An array of ten integers
myArray[0] = −5; // Set the first integer in the array to −5
```

An associative container, on the other hand, can use any data type to reference the items in the container. For example, you might choose to use a `string` to reference a collection of `int` items to store a list of students' ages according to their names.

```
std :: map<std :: string, int> students;
```

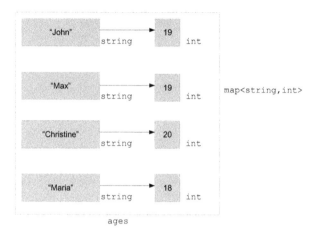

Figure 23.1: Pairing `strings` and `ints` in a `map` object

Perhaps you want to create the object with some initial values:

```
std :: map<std :: string , int > students =
   { {"John" ,  19},
     {"Max" ,  19},
     {"Christine" ,  20},
     {"Maria" ,  18} };
```

This code produces a structure like in Figure 23.1. With these names and ages paired, we can now retrieve the ages using the names.

```
string  name  =  "Christine";
std :: cout << name <<  " is  " << students [name]
   << " years  old." << std :: endl ;

// This code  prints :
// Christine  is  20  years  old .
```

New students may also be added in the following way:

```
students ["June"]  =  18;
students ["Omar"]  =  19;
```

Objects of type map may be iterated, and in C++11, their contents can be printed in a range-based for loop as we briefly demonstrate here. Each item in the std::map<std::string, int> is of type std::pair<std::string,int>.

```cpp
for (auto& item : students)
{
  std::cout << item.first << " is " << item.second << "
      years old." << std::endl;
}

// This code prints:
// John is 19 years old
// Max is 19 years old
// Christine is 20 years old
// Maria is 18 years old
// June is 18 years old
// Omar is 19 years old
```

23.5 Further Reading

- http://en.wikipedia.org/wiki/Standard_Template_Library
- http://www.cplusplus.com/reference/stl/

Index